Prayer
STORM

Prayer STORM

THE HOUR THAT CHANGES THE WORLD

JAMES W. GOLL

DESTINY IMAGE® PUBLISHERS, INC.
PO Box 310, Shippensburg, PA 17257-0310

*"Speaking to the Purposes of God for This Generation
and for the Generations to Come."*

This book and all other Destiny Image, Revival Press, MercyPlace, Fresh Bread, Destiny Image Fiction, and Treasure House books are available at Christian bookstores and distributors worldwide.

For a U.S. bookstore nearest you, call 1-800-722-6774.
For more information on foreign distributors, call 717-532-3040.
Reach us on the Internet at www.destinyimage.com.

ISBN 10: 0-7684-2716-9
ISBN 13: 978-0-7684-2716-5

For Worldwide Distribution, Printed in the U.S.A.

DEDICATION

As a student of Church history and one who loves prayer and its role in world missions, I dedicate this book to the legacy of Count Nicolas Ludwig von Zinzendorf, Christian David, Anna Nitschmann, and the other early leaders of the group that eventually became known as the Moravians. I have been impacted immeasurably by the shadow of the Lord Jesus that they cast. It is an honor to be one of the many intercessors who today have picked up the baton of prayer that the Moravian believers so faithfully carried for well over a hundred years.

ACKNOWLEDGMENTS

With deep, heart-felt gratitude, I wish to thank the team of people at Encounters Network and Destiny Image who made this project possible. I especially want to recognize Kathy Deering as one of the best writing editors I have ever met. It is an honor to work with her.

I also want to say "thank you" to the Holy Spirit for giving me a dream concerning the Prayer Storm and to the Lord for trusting me with a commission to this great task. Thanks to all the prayer warriors who have already joined us in this "hour that changes the world" and to all of you who, after reading this book, will be ready to join in. Together, in Jesus, we make a great team!

ENDORSEMENTS

My dear friend James Goll has been given a mandate that all of us have been called to participate in. It is a call to perpetual unceasing prayer...sounds like God to me. God has given James many prophetic visions and dreams; this one could not have come at a more crucial time in our culture and in our history. The Church is in desperate need of authenticity and relevance...we will find it first on our faces before God. The youth of the world are being visited by God in a fresh way. This will intensify as we pray because the demonic attack against the youth of our generation is unprecedented, and we need to push back the forces of darkness. The descendants of Abraham are in need of Messiah; our prayers on their behalf and our intercession will make a difference. And finally, the world is in a state of turmoil, upheaval, and crisis; only prayer changes the destiny of nations. Our mandate is James' mandate...the Moravian Lampstand must be restored. Once again, my deepest thanks to a man of his word, a man of God's Word, and my brother in arms, James Goll, for being brave enough and bold enough to call us to our highest place of power...our knees!

Dr. Mark J. Chironna
The Master's Touch International Church
Mark Chironna Ministries
Orlando, Florida

James Goll has done it again! His new book, *Prayer Storm*, is a spiritual manual for every Christian, whether new to prayer or an experienced intercessor. This textbook probes the spirit of the early Moravian intercessors and casts a vision for rekindling their powerful lamp into our dark world. James has provided us with principles and sound doctrine, but he also gives us sample prayers and guidelines to become part of a global prayer storm. We learn how to conspire with God to bring His will to come on this earth. We find out how to pray with God instead of praying to God.

James is not starting a new organization that replicates other prayer ministries, but he provides the connecting lines between the dots of intercession around the world. I encourage every Christian to not just read the text contained within this book's pages but to actively participate in a prayer movement that will change our globe.

Harry R. Jackson Jr.
Senior Pastor, Hope Christian Church
Founder and President, High Impact Leadership Coalition
Washington, D.C.

In his newest book, James Goll issues an urgent challenge to every believer to be part of spiritual "crisis intervention" at this critical juncture in history. Through a dream, God revealed a vision and strategy for a worldwide, corporate call to consistent, persistent prayer—Prayer Storm—that will intervene and change things in the earth realm. Four specific areas are targeted for focused prayer. I encourage you to get this book: read it, sign up, and *pray*!

Jane Hansen Hoyt
President/CEO, Aglow International
Edmonds, Washington

I am passionately excited about Jim Goll's powerful book, *Prayer Storm*, that I believe God will use to transform the global prayer movement. Nothing I know of will impact the nations for Jesus Christ like restoring the Moravian Prayer Watch as described in Goll's inspired and anointed call to continuous prayer. Our ministry, Every Home for Christ, wants to be first in line to partner with Jim in this global call to continuous prayer.

Dr. Dick Eastman
International President
Every Home for Christ and
President of America's National
Prayer Committee

A Global Prayer Army is arising in this hour across the face of the earth to lay seize to the kingdom of darkness by penetrating it with the arsenal of worship and intercession. I encourage you to join in the strategic ministry of James W. Goll and countless others worldwide in the Prayer Storm efforts to keep the fire continually burning on the altar. May the fire of the Lord burn on your heart as you read this contagious book.

Lou Engle
Director of The Call

With a passion for prayer and the purposes of God, James Goll brings us additional needed tools for the global prayer army for these Last Days. I exhort you to be a practical part of the worldwide prayer movement and consider joining James Goll and thousands of others in the hour that changes the world.

Mike Bickle
International House of Prayer of Kansas City
Author of Passion of Jesus and many others

The time is now! The Holy Spirit is sounding an alarm across the Body of Christ to awaken believers to our God-given position of authority to make history through the power of prevailing prayer. Join James Goll in "the hour that changes the world." It is time to mount the walls of intercession!

Cindy Jacobs
Cofounder of Generals International
International Director of the Deborah
Company and Reformation Prayer Network

God's heart cry is that His people stand united as watchmen together in this critical hour of history. Join James Goll, myself, and thousands of others as we lift our voices for the youth, Israel, and the church. We need a revival that brings reformation, and only sustained, united prayer will bring this about!

Robert Stearns
Founder of Eagles Wings
Cochairman, Day of Prayer for the Peace of Jerusalem

The key to sustained revival that transforms society is the power of enduring prayer. The teaching and the applications of *Prayer Storm* will help the global army of intercessors stay focused and targeted in their prayer efforts. Don't just read another book—do what this book says. Have a life full of life-altering intercession.

Dutch Sheets
Senior Leader of Freedom Church
Founder of USAAN
Author of *Intercessory Prayer, Watchmen Prayer and Praying for America*

CONTENTS

FOREWORD

Prayer Storm may well turn out to be one of the most significant messages to the Body of Christ in this season. I will explain so that you will be able to see this book in its full context.

The biblical agenda item that God has been pushing to the top of the priority list of Christian leaders nationally and internationally during this season has been the "Dominion Mandate." Think about Adam and Eve. After God had created all the incredible things on earth, He climaxed it with creating human beings in His own image. Why did God create humans? He created humans so they would take charge of all the rest of creation. God specifically said that Adam and Eve should "take dominion" over what He had put on earth (see Genesis 1:26,28). This is where the term Dominion Mandate originates.

Keep in mind that *Adam* is not only the name of a person, but in Hebrew it means "the human race." You and I were not in the Garden of Eden personally, but we were there genetically because we all have some of Adam's DNA. When Adam acted, he acted not only on his own behalf, but in the broad sense, on our behalf as well. As we know, he definitely made the wrong choice.

Satan knew that God had given Adam the authority to take dominion and also the authority to give dominion away.

Satan tempted Adam because he wanted to regain the authority he lost when he was cast out of Heaven. Adam yielded to temptation; he chose to obey satan rather than God, and from that point on satan usurped Adam's rightful dominion and began to have his way in the world, which is to steal, kill, and destroy. That is why satan is called "the god of this age" and "the prince of the power of the air" (see Eph. 2:2).

But this was not and never has been God's plan for life on earth. God turned things around by sending the Second Adam, Jesus Christ. Jesus came to destroy the works of satan, namely to begin the process of taking back the dominion that Adam had given away in the Garden. Jesus sent His disciples out to preach the gospel of the kingdom. *Kingdom* means dominion because it has two parts: *king* and *dom,* which are the first three letters of the word *dominion.* A king has dominion over a realm. Jesus is the King and His realm is the earth. Jesus paid the price for retaking dominion by His death and resurrection. But when He left the earth, He said that we, His disciples, would receive power when the Holy Spirit comes, in order to be His witnesses. What does this mean? Implementing the Dominion Mandate is our responsibility as Jesus' representatives in this season.

Which brings me to the crucial importance of *Prayer Storm.*

James Goll knows and teaches everything I have just said. One thing he knows very well is that when Jesus came to bring His kingdom, He was invading the kingdom that satan had dominated since the time of Adam. What does this mean? It means war! Satan never lets go of any territory he has occupied without a fight. As Jesus' witnesses, it is our responsibility to engage satan and fight this war under the power of the Holy Spirit on Jesus' behalf. The war will not be over until God's people regain their rightful dominion over creation and Jesus turns the kingdom over to His Father as it says in First Corinthians 15:24.

If we are going to win this war, our first weapon must be prayer. I am not referring to the traditional, routine, plain vanilla, religious prayer that most Christians are used to. I mean an extraordinary level of prayer—a battle-winning, world-changing kind of prayer. I mean prayer that will defeat the enemy in your personal life as well as in your church life, as well as seeing the community in which you live transformed for God!

How do we get to this level of prayer? James Goll has drawn on his extensive experience, his profound knowledge of the Word of God, and his fine-tuned spiritual discernment to give us definitive answers to this question in *Prayer Storm*. Yes, *Prayer Storm* is one of the most significant messages to the Body of Christ for this season. As you read, you will find your place in serving God during the wonderful times in which we live!

C. Peter Wagner, Presiding Apostle
International Coalition of Apostles

Introduction

Restoring the Global Moravian Lampstand

In the spring of 2007, I had a vivid dream. I would call it a "commissioning dream," because, in this dream, I heard an audible voice utter these words: "I commission you to restore and release the global Moravian lampstand!" With that imperative sentence ringing in my ears, I woke up. There in my bedroom, in amber-colored letters, I saw two words written out in front of my eyes: *Prayer Storm.*

I was fully awake. Suddenly it was as if God's Spirit downloaded into my spirit what this meant. Intuitively, I knew that Prayer Storm would be a worldwide call to consistent, persistent prayer and that it would involve four expressions of prayer. Prayer Storm would focus on three particular areas, vitally undergirded by a fourth. Prayer Storm would involve prayer for (1) revival in the Church, (2) the greatest youth awakening that the world has ever seen, and (3) Israel, all the descendants of Abraham. These prayers would be strengthened by widespread, well-coordinated intercession for (4) God's intervention in times of major crisis.

Urgent Attention

I sensed an urgency in the voice of the Lord as His words were engraved upon my soul. This was important to Him. This undertaking needed immediate attention. My calling as a watchman on the wall had been renewed instantly, and I needed to respond, like Esther, "for such a time as this" (Esther 4:14). It was all here:

Commission, restoration, release...

The Moravian lampstand...

Revival, Youth, Israel, Crisis Intervention...

It would be a Prayer Storm.

This was not a commissioning for one man; it was a commissioning for many people, for the task of orchestrating a worldwide symphony of worship and prayer that would play an essential part in winning for the Lamb the world that He had suffered and died for. My role would be to implement whatever He showed me. Each person who became involved would have a particular part to play.

I knew that God was restoring one more aspect of the watch of the Lord. The prayer movement, which has had many expressions over the past couple of decades, was being further expanded. Prayer Storm was supposed to become one more part of the divine tapestry of the prayer movement, with its definite distinctions but unified goal. It wouldn't replace or compete with any of the other expressions of prayer that have been established, such as 24/7 houses of prayer, prayer mountains, prophetic declarations, or various types of global networks and outreaches. No, far from being a competitor, Prayer Storm would take its place on the spiritual battlefield, shoulder-to-shoulder with the other endeavors that God has already raised up, including the local church. We would all be able to collaborate. With an increasingly effective Internet presence, Prayer Storm could become an international, virtual house of prayer.

"Could You Not Watch With Me One Hour?"

Immediately after that dream, our Encounters Network staff and I began to swing into action. We set up a Web site right away (www.prayerstorm.com). We began to expand on each of the four categories of prayer and to make it possible for people to sign up for specific times of prayer. It went live in January of 2008.

One hour per person per week—that is all it takes to keep the watch going. It doesn't matter what time zone a person lives in. A global house of prayer spans all of them, so no one hour period receives heavier coverage than another. (We decided to coordinate it all from the central time zone of the United States, but that's only for the sake of establishing a reference point for keeping track of how many people are praying at any given hour around the world.)

Those who sign up do not have to attend a particular meeting, although they may wish to pray in the context of a meeting that they already have established. People don't have to stop any other prayer endeavor they are already committed to in order to participate in this one. People can pray from their homes. Prayer Storm has a simple and flexible format.

In the Garden of Gethsemane, Jesus said to Peter and the other disciples, "Could you not watch with me one hour" (Matt. 26:40 NKJV). I hear Him asking each one of us that question. Can you watch with Him one hour? Prayer Storm can help you do it. Prayer Storm might just become the hour that changes the world!

The 100-Year Prayer Meeting

Now let's go back to the Moravians. In 1722, Count Nicolas Ludwig von Zinzendorf was asked by a group of Christians if they could cross the border from Moravia in order to live on his lands. He assented, and they settled in a town they called *Herrnhut*, which means "the Lord's Watch." Zinzendorf had always been interested in a life of prayer and devotion to God, and after his tenants suffered a season of prolonged disagreement and difficulty, he began to lead daily Bible studies for them in 1727. A sudden time of revival occurred, which many have called "the Moravian Pentecost." The effects of this move of the Holy Spirit have been far-reaching, indeed.

One of the first results of the revival was that 24 men and 24 women covenanted to devote one hour every day to concerted prayer. It was a very simple model, and soon others joined them. This was the beginning of what became a 100-year-long prayer watch. Every hour of every day, someone was praying. While others were working, someone was praying. They prayed 24 hours a day, 7 days a week, 365 days a year. The "altar fire" never went out. The Moravians cited one Scripture passage in particular as their inspiration: "The fire shall ever be burning upon the altar; it shall never go out" (Lev. 6:13 KJV).

These men and women were young. Even their patron, Count Zinzendorf, was only 27 years old at the beginning. Almost immediately, they began to launch evangelistic missions to foreign lands as far-flung as the West Indies, Greenland and Lapland, and Turkey. As the years passed, they grew old and passed the baton to others; Zinzendorf died in 1760. But the prayer continued unabated.

By 1792, 65 years after the prayer watch began, that one small band of Moravian believers had sent 300 missionaries to all parts of the globe. The fire had indeed remained lit on the Moravian lampstand, and from it, the light of the Kingdom had illuminated thousands of dark hearts. The world would never be the same.

As the Moravians went off to other lands, they came to the notice of other Christians, and their reputation for trustful faith and evangelistic results spread. Of particular note is John Wesley, who first encountered some Moravians on his return from a missionary venture to the American colonies in 1736. The faith-filled, worshipful demeanor of the Moravian believers, who were sometimes known as the Happy People or the Easter People, impressed him so greatly that soon afterward he sought and attained an experience of having his heart "strangely warmed" by the love of the Holy Spirit. Wesley later visited Herrnhut and observed their community life, where no one worked unless someone else was praying, and he wrote, in a letter to Count Zinzendorf, "When will this Christianity cover the earth as the waters cover the seas?"[1]

PRACTICAL TOOLS

Praying an hour a week doesn't sound like much, but we all know that it's not easy to remember to do it, let alone to do it effectively. It's especially difficult to sustain such a commitment over a long stretch of time.

To rally intercessors around the world, we intend to supply a number of practical tools. The book you are holding is one of them, as well as the corresponding Study Guide and the DVD and CD sets of teachings. These tools will help you catch the vision and run with it, giving you something to learn from and to refer back to.

Another practical tool is our weekly e-mail communication, which is specific to Prayer Storm. I want to give you teaching and insight on a regular basis. In addition, we release prayer news bulletins when a significant crisis occurs somewhere in the world, such as a natural disaster or a violent military uprising or an alarming political development. We have also launched our weekly Prayer Storm web-based TV show—I will exhort you, and we will actually intercede together. And that's just for starters! Through all of the crisis praying, I want to be able to keep us focused, though, on praying for revival in the Church, a youth awakening, and Israel, on an on-going basis.

You can pray all by yourself, or you can incorporate this model into your existing house of prayer or church prayer ministry. We will participate in established efforts such as the Global Bridegroom Fast that Mike Bickle coordinates from IHOP in Kansas City and TheCall efforts around the globe with Lou Engle. We will inform our community of intercessors, via our mailing list, whenever the Spirit initiates something new that we feel we should participate in. We want to respond to the progressive vision as it unfolds and to make it possible for you to respond to God's call.

WHAT IS THE "MORAVIAN LAMPSTAND"?

Concerted, sustained prayer of this nature has happened in the past (usually without the Internet component, of course). One of those past events furnishes us with the term "Moravian lampstand."

In 1727, in Herrnhut, Saxony, under the leadership of Count Nicolas Ludwig von Zinzendorf, night-and-day intercession arose in a small community in what today is eastern Germany. The people in the community had come from Moravia, so they became known as the Moravians. This prayer vigil continued for *over 110 years*, and it fueled a missionary movement that touched the world. The men and women of Herrnhut committed themselves to hourly intercession in order to, in their words, "win for the Lamb the rewards of His suffering." I will come back to the Moravians in a moment, after I mention a few other Spirit-inspired prayer surges that occurred both before and after the Moravians.

Earliest of all, we know about the Tabernacle of David in Jerusalem at about 1000 B.C. Under the leadership of King David and his son Solomon (both of whom had a revelatory understanding of the importance of continual prayer), organized worship and prayer continued for 33 years nonstop, night-and-day. To make it possible, David and Solomon financed full-time singers and musicians (see 1 Chron. 9:33; 15:16; 23:5; 25:7; 2 Chron. 5:12-13). The Scriptures prophetically declare that, in the future, there will be a restoration of David's tabernacle (see Amos 9:11).

Even a thousand years later, in the time of the Book of Acts, the Jews had what they called "hours of prayer," and the Christians carried on with the tradition. These were set times of day when believers would gather together to pray. (See Acts 3:1; 16:13.)

God revived the idea of continual, committed prayer in Ireland in A.D. 555 under the leadership of Comgall, who was the senior abbot of the great monastery at Bangor, and later under his disciple Columbanus. Bangor became the site where night-and-day worship with prayers continued for over 300 years, fueling a missionary zeal that touched all of Europe.

Jumping to the present, we can't ignore one well-known move of prayer in South Korea known as the Prayer Mountain, established in 1973 by David Yonggi Cho as part of the Yoido Full Gospel Church. Again, missionary work is the focus, particularly throughout Asia. The Prayer Mountain, which is an actual mountain, has facilities for up to 10,000 people, including special cubicles where prayer warriors can spend prolonged periods of time fasting, praying, and seeking God's will. Among the many obvious results of their prayers, we see the phenomenal growth of their church. When their church reached the record-breaking size of 700,000 members, Dr. Cho decided that they would start planting churches and establishing satellite churches, which they have continued to do as they grow.

In every case, we see that the result of sustained prayer—often coupled with worship—is amazing growth and expansion of the Kingdom of God and the Church. In the latter part of the 20th century, and now in the 21st century, God has been restoring night-and-day worship and prayer in many cities and nations of the earth as part of His commitment to release in these last days an outpouring of His Spirit. These places and ministries include, but are not limited to: the International House of Prayer in Kansas City, Missouri, (Mike Bickle) and associated locations throughout the world; The Jerusalem House of Prayer for All Nations on the Mount of Olives (Tom Hess); The Watch of the Lord in Charlotte, North Carolina (Mahesh and Bonnie Chavda); the Governmental Prayer Alliance in Colorado Springs, Colorado (Dutch Sheets); the Reformation Prayer Network, Red Oak, Texas (Cindy Jacobs); the 24/7 Prayer Movement based in England (Pete Greig); as well as the International Fellowship of Intercessors, with "first Friday" prayer and fasting for governmental bodies in various countries (Gary Bergel is the U.S. director). This sampling is, by no means, a complete listing of the various voices that are currently contributing to the concert of prayer in the world today.

RE-IGNITING THE MORAVIAN LAMPSTAND

Here we are today, at the beginning of the 21st century, and more and more groups of "Moravians" are catching the vision for sustained prayer, worship, and intercession, for 24/7, unceasing prayer for cities, nations, and the entire globe. I believe that

Prayer Storm will raise one more unified, God-ordained voice in the worldwide chorus.

A Prayer Storm is on the horizon, and we will be the Storm Warriors. We're going to be prayer warriors who pray in the storm. We're going to pray God's thunder, because God's voice thunders.

> *Listen closely to the thunder of His voice, and the rumbling that goes out from His mouth. Under the whole heaven He lets it loose, and His lightning to the ends of the earth. After it, a voice roars; He thunders with His majestic voice, and He does not restrain the lightnings when His voice is heard. God thunders with His voice wondrously, doing great things which we cannot comprehend* (Job 37:2-5).

Don't you want to be a part of God's Prayer Storm army? Then read on—this was written just for you!

Part I

VISION FOR A PRAYER STORM

Sweet Hour of Prayer

Sweet hour of prayer! sweet hour of prayer!
That calls me from a world of care,
And bids me at my Father's throne
Make all my wants and wishes known.
In seasons of distress and grief,
My soul has often found relief
And oft escaped the tempter's snare
By thy return, sweet hour of prayer!

Sweet hour of prayer! sweet hour of prayer!
The joys I feel, the bliss I share,
Of those whose anxious spirits burn
With strong desires for thy return!
With such I hasten to the place
Where God my Savior shows His face,
And gladly take my station there,
And wait for thee, sweet hour of prayer!

Sweet hour of prayer! sweet hour of prayer!
Thy wings shall my petition bear
To Him whose truth and faithfulness
Engage the waiting soul to bless.
And since He bids me seek His face,
Believe His Word and trust His grace,
I'll cast on Him my every care,
And wait for thee, sweet hour of prayer![1]

Chapter 1

"PRAYER STORM"—WHAT IS IT?

As I looked, behold, a stormy wind came out of the north, and a great cloud with a fire enveloping it and flashing continually; a brightness was about it and out of the midst of it there seemed to glow amber metal, out of the midst of the fire (Ezekiel 1:4 AMP).

When I woke up from the commissioning dream about the Moravian lampstand, and I saw the glowing, amber words, *Prayer Storm*, emblazoned in front of my eyes, not only did I understand instantly that God wanted me to orchestrate a move of prayer, I also knew that *storm* would be a key word—and an actual experience—all the way through.

The *prayer* part was not a new idea. Dictionary definitions concur that *prayer* is an earnest, heartfelt request made before God (or a godlike authority). But the definition of *storm* gets more interesting. What is a storm? A natural storm involves a disturbance in the air above the earth. It includes strong winds, sometimes lightening and thunder, and often some form of precipitation, such as rain, snow, sleet, or hail. Already, this makes me think of a number of Scriptures that paint a vivid picture of God's power sweeping down on the earth. Turn the page back to Job 37:2–5, at the end of the introduction, and then look below at a few more:

See, the storm of the Lord will burst out in wrath, a whirl-wind swirling down on the heads of the wicked. The anger of the Lord will not turn back until He fully accomplishes the purposes of His heart. In days to come you will under-stand it clearly (Jeremiah 23:19-20 NIV).

Like fire that burns the forest and like a flame that sets the mountains on fire, so pursue them with Your tempest and terrify them with Your storm (Psalm 83:14-15).

The Lord is slow to anger and great in power; the Lord will not leave the guilty unpunished. His way is in the whirl-wind and the storm, and clouds are the dust of His feet (Nahum 1:3 NIV).

He covers His hands with the lightning, and commands it to strike the mark (Job 36:32).

God not only commands natural storms on the earth, He is a storm. And by extension, since we have been created in His image, commissioned as His servants, and adopted as sons, we are like storms too, when we are acting in His name. That last passage (Job 36:32) says that He covers His hands with lightning and sends it forth to strike the mark. When we pray to Him, we're calling forth the storm of God to invade the earth realm. We're drawing His attention to a particular "mark" or target.

We can't see the spiritual storm that rages in mid-heaven, although it is spoken about in the Bible. (See Daniel 7–9, for example.) But God is looking for people to join their voices in prayer so that He can release the angelic host to do battle all the more. He wants to hear the prayers of people on earth so that He can release the winds of His Spirit and the rain of His justice.

A storm of prayer releases a storm of power. A prayer storm, to pull out some more dictionary definitions of *storm,* does not have to be compared only with weather terminology. You can have other kinds of storms: a storm of anger or protest; or a storm of the opposite emotion, such as a storm of laughter; a storm or bombardment of objects, a storm or torrent of communications, even a storm *window* (we could play with that one!). When we use the word *storm* as a verb, we talk about military-type storming of a fortified location, often suddenly and with great force, in order to attack and capture it. We speak of storming out of a room with violent anger, pushing forward like a thunderhead driven before the wind. We also, of course, say it is "storming" when the sky is dark, lightening flashes, and the wind blows, driving rain or snow before it.[2]

So what is a prayer storm? A *prayer storm* is when people cry out, not just quietly but in a passionate, verbal way, asking God, in the name of Jesus, to change things. We are calling forth the strong winds of the Spirit and the glorious flashings of His brilliant presence. We want Him to shatter the darkness with His light. We are holding up targets for Him to aim at. "Come, Lord! Come here to my city. Storm the gates! Blow us out of our comfortable traditions. Break off our blinders. Strike our enemies. Win back Your people."

PRAYER OF INTERCESSION

Except in the context of prayer, we rarely use the words *intercession* and *intercede*. The term is a little old-fashioned for contemporary, everyday conversation. But it's a great word that conveys exactly the right meaning when we're talking about a prayer storm.

Intercede comes from two Latin words, *inter* and *cedere*. *Inter* means "between, among, involved." Think of the word *intervention*. *Cedere* means "to yield, to go or to move, or to pray the price of."[3] So when we intercede in prayer, we go between—almost like stepping between someone and an enemy. We yield ourselves, humbling ourselves to assist those who are weak and who need help. We move in the direction of involvement regarding the hurts and needs of other people, as the Good Samaritan did (see Luke 10:33). As we are moved upon and as we move both in prayer and in action, we *intercede*.

Prayer moves us toward God and toward other people. We see God's righteousness on the one hand and people's state of abject sin on the other, and we want to help pay the price for their salvation and freedom. We want to be go-betweens. We act between parties with a view to reconcile those who differ or contend with each other. We mediate. We make entreaties. In a word, we *intercede*.

Intercession is a holy act of prayer through which we call forth reconciliation between opposing parties, whether that means between God and a particular person, between God and a city, between God and a nation, or between two human beings such as father and son, husband and wife, or brother and sister. Intercessory prayer is a high calling, a calling that is meant for every one of us.

When you intercede, you stand in the gap. It's as if you create a pause in the commotion, an atmospheric shift that temporarily holds tumult at bay so that the voice of the Lord can be released. His conviction can settle on hearts. His promises can find fulfillment in an individual life, in a city, or in a region. "Thy Kingdom come; Thy will be done in earth as it is in heaven" (Matt. 6:10 KJV). We become conduits for Kingdom activity. We move and speak and stand for God in the times in which we find ourselves.

When we intercede, we mediate between two extremes, between parties who are at variance with each other. We bring peace. We do it through prayer, calling forth peace where there is war and conflict. I'm not referring only to times of literal war or to crisis intervention but also to "wars of the soul." When you see someone whose soul is in a state of war, in conflict with God's will, your prayers can make a difference. You can call on God to bring that person into the eye in the middle of the storm, that center of perfect peace. There all friction, warfare, and tumult are pushed aside, at least temporarily, creating a divine opportunity for the human will or the governing authorities of a city, region, or nation to respond to God's invitation.

BIBLICAL USAGE

In the New Testament, the word *intercede* (or *intercession*) is used four specific times. It's used twice in Romans 8 and once each in Hebrews 7 and First Timothy 2:

> *In the same way the Spirit also helps our weakness; for we do not know how to pray as we should, but the Spirit Himself intercedes for us with groanings too deep for words; and He who searches the hearts knows what the mind of the Spirit is, because He intercedes for the saints according to the will of God* (Romans 8:26-27).

> *Therefore He is able also to save forever those who draw near to God through Him, since He always lives to make intercession for them* (Hebrews 7:25).

> *I exhort, therefore, that, first of all, supplications, prayers, intercessions, and giving of thanks be made for all men; for kings, and for all that are in authority, that we may lead a quiet and peaceable life in all godliness and reverence* (1 Timothy 2:1-2 NKJV).

The Spirit helps our weakness, as we see in Romans 8:26, as we yield ourselves to Him. His Spirit is within us, and He will intercede in us and through us. He will locate the places of weakness where we truly do not know how to pray as we ought, and He will release prayers that go beyond our natural, limited understanding and information. As we yield to Him, He will pray from a revelatory dimension. Some of the prayers will be beyond the articulation of natural speech.

Jesus ever lives to make intercession, and Jesus' Spirit lives in us. Therefore, Jesus has an ongoing ministry in and through us. His ministry has not ceased just because He is out of our sight. He continues to intercede from the right hand of God the Father, and He continues to intercede through us here on earth. He always lives to make intercession. He intercedes. He's standing in the gap as our Living Sacrifice, our Savior. In our exhortations to each other to pray, we like to talk about the importance of "two or three" coming into agreement: "Again, I tell you that if two of you on earth agree about anything you ask for, it will be done for you by my Father in heaven. For where two or three come together in my name, there am I with them" (Matt. 18:19-20 NIV).

But I'll tell you the main person you have to come into agreement with—God. If you come into agreement with God, His Holy Spirit will intercede through you, and your prayers *will* be answered. Jesus' role is to intercede, and our role is to come into agreement with Him, with the attitude of thanksgiving. This precludes disagreement and criticism, and it prevents discernment from being turned into accusation. So the Holy Spirit intercedes. Jesus intercedes. And each one of us intercedes. There's your "two or three" right there! Let's get those three in agreement together, and we'll have a three-cord strand that will not be quickly torn apart (see Eccles. 4:12).

INSIGHT FROM GREEK AND HEBREW

In the Greek lexicon, we find a couple of definitions of *intercede* that help us understand the word. The first definition is "to light upon a person or a thing, to fall in with, to hit upon a person or a thing, to chance upon something, to encounter unexpectedly."[4] A second definition is "to go to or to meet a person, especially for conversation or consultation."[5]

Both of these definitions help round out our appreciation for the richness of the word *intercede*. The Holy Spirit will "light upon" you. He will come upon you. At times, you will have unexpected encounters with Him. He will talk with you, and you can talk with Him.

The Hebrew word for intercession is *paga*, which is defined as meaning, "to meet; to light upon (by chance); to fall upon, attack, strike down, cut down; to strike the mark; to be laid upon."[6] The Hebrew word is used in Isaiah 64:5, which is about a meeting with God for the purpose of reconciliation:

> *You meet and spare him who joyfully works righteousness (uprightness and justice), [earnestly] remembering You in Your ways. Behold, You were angry, for we sinned; we have long continued in our sins [prolonging Your anger]. And shall we be saved?* (Isaiah 64:5 AMP).

It is also used in Genesis 26:10-17 in the sense of "to light upon," to indicate how God's grace works; our divine Helper is standing by, ready to aid us in our intercession, moving us from our natural ability to His supernatural ability, from our finite ability to His infinite ability, taking hold of our situation with us so as to accomplish the will of God.

Paga is used also in First Samuel 22 and Second Samuel 1 in the sense of falling upon, attacking, striking down, cutting down. This shows us that the word *intercession* can carry a warfare connotation, indicating the readiness of a soldier to fall upon or attack the enemy at the word of his commander, striking the mark (remember the lightning strikes of Job 36:32) and cutting down the enemy. God is looking throughout the earth for targets to send the light of His glory to, and we are the ones who get to paint the targets for God!

You can paint targets on your city; you can paint them on your congregation; you can paint them on the lost; you can paint them on your spouse—whatever He shows you. This is not witchcraft praying, praying for bad things to happen. This is Holy Ghost desperation, saying "Oh, God! Come! Help!"

Intercession reached its fullest and most profound expression when our sins were "laid upon" Jesus. Jesus was able to identify fully with us when the totality of our human condition was placed upon Him, and then, as the scapegoat, He carried it far away. As His Body, we can enter into this aspect of intercession when we, as Colossians 1:24 calls us to do, share on behalf of His Body (which is the Church), filling up that which is lacking in Christ's afflictions: "Now I rejoice in my sufferings for your sake, and in my flesh I do my share on behalf of His body, which is the church, in filling up what is lacking in Christ's afflictions" (Col. 1:24).

Doing that kind of intercession doesn't mean that we have a "messianic complex" or that we're repeating something that Jesus has already done. It just means that His burden comes over us and that we are privileged to carry it with Him. We are graced to participate in the desires of His heart. Like the Moravians of old, we want to see Jesus receive the rewards of His suffering, and we step into a revelation of our priestly privilege before Him.

Kingdom of Priests

We are part of the priesthood of all believers, and we serve each other and Him as priests. Following Old Testament typology, we can apply present meanings to the priestly duty of burning incense on the altar of incense (which are spelled-out in the following passages) as we offer up fragrant prayers that have been skillfully blended together according to His instructions:

Moreover, you shall make an altar as a place for burning incense;…Aaron shall burn fragrant incense on it; he shall burn it every morning when he trims the lamps. When Aaron trims the lamps at twilight, he shall burn incense. There shall be perpetual incense before the Lord throughout your generations. You shall not offer any strange incense on this altar, or burnt offering or meal offering (Exodus 30:1,7-9).

Then the Lord said to Moses, "Take for yourself spices, stacte and onycha and galbanum, spices with pure frankincense; there shall be an equal part of each. With it you shall make incense, a perfume, the work of a perfumer, salted, pure, and holy" (Exodus 30:34-35).

Aaron shall enter the holy place with this: with a bull for a sin offering and a ram for a burnt offering….He shall take a firepan full of coals of fire from upon the altar before the Lord and two handfuls of finely ground sweet incense, and bring it inside the veil (Leviticus 16:3,12).

Following are the verses that dictated to Israel how they were to handle the sacrificial offerings:

Command Aaron and his sons, saying, "This is the law for the burnt offering: the burnt offering itself shall remain on the hearth on the altar all night until the morning, and the

— 39 —

fire on the altar is to be kept burning on it. The priest is to put on his linen robe, and he shall put on undergarments next to his flesh; and he shall take up the ashes to which the fire reduces the burnt offering on the altar and place them beside the altar. Then he shall take off his garments and put on other garments, and carry the ashes outside the camp to a clean place. The fire on the altar shall be kept burning on it. It shall not go out, but the priest shall burn wood on it every morning; and he shall lay out the burnt offering on it, and offer up in smoke the fat portions of the peace offerings on it. Fire shall be kept burning continually on the altar; it is not to go out (Leviticus 6:9-13).

Verse 13 is the one that inspired Count Zinzendorf and others to initiate the Moravian prayer meeting that lasted over a hundred years: "Fire shall be kept burning continually on the altar; it is not to go out."

Later we read about how Moses told Aaron to make atonement for the people with incense:

Moses said to Aaron, "Take your censer and put in it fire from the altar, and lay incense on it; then bring it quickly to the congregation and make atonement for them, for wrath has gone forth from the Lord, the plague has begun!" Then Aaron took it as Moses had spoken, and ran into the midst of the assembly, for behold, the plague had begun among the people. So he put on the incense and made atonement for the people. He took his stand between the dead and the living, so that the plague was checked (Numbers 16:46-48).

This is a perfect picture of crisis intercession. With his censor of burning incense, Aaron ran between the dead and the living and stopped the plague that was killing the people. Close to 15,000 people had already died from the plague, but when he waved the incense in his censor, death was halted and life prevailed. In the same way, life comes from the fragrant incense of our obedient prayers.

Today, we are no longer limited to a handful of special actions by designated priestly intermediaries in a circumscribed locality. No, as we read in First Peter 2:9 and Revelation 1:6 and 5:10, we are a royal priesthood. That term is all-inclusive—*we* does not mean only the pastors or special people—it means you and me. We aren't limited to a particular structure called a tabernacle, because the Holy Spirit is tabernacled within our hearts:

But you are a chosen people, a royal priesthood, a holy nation, a people belonging to God, that you may declare the praises of him who called you out of darkness into his wonderful light (1 Peter 2:9 NIV).

He has made us to be a kingdom, priests to His God and Father—to Him be the glory and the dominion forever and ever. Amen (Revelation 1:6).

You have made them to be a kingdom and priests to serve our God, and they will reign on the earth (Revelation 5:10 NIV).

So we keep the altar of incense burning continually, just as the priests did. The only thing that is different is that our altar of incense is within our own hearts. We offer up spiritual sacrifices in the spirit of Hebrews 13:15: "…praise to God…the fruit of lips that give thanks to His name." We "enter His gates with thanksgiving, and His courts with praise…" (Ps. 100:4). We know about the golden harp and golden bowl upon the altar of Heaven, where the incense is the prayers of the saints, filling the bowl, and the harp is the ministry of praise and worship (see

Rev. 5:8). As we watch, an angel takes his censor, fills it with the fire from the heavenly altar, and casts it down onto the earth (see Rev. 8:4-5). We keep our fire of prayer burning on the altar of our hearts, and the heavenly altar fire burns all the more brightly. We stir ourselves up, and we join ourselves with others who likewise have a passion for the fire of the Lord. We pour our hearts out in worship, praise, adoration, and love and, like Aaron the priest, we go out and take a stand between the living and the dead.

THE INCENSE OF PRAYER

God instructed Moses about how to make the fragrant incense that was supposed to be burned on the altar of incense:

> *Then the Lord said to Moses, "Take for yourself spices, stacte and onycha and galbanum, spices with pure frankincense; there shall be an equal part of each. With it you shall make incense, a perfume, the work of a perfumer, salted, pure, and holy. You shall beat some of it very fine, and put part of it before the testimony in the tent of meeting where I will meet with you; it shall be most holy to you. The incense which you shall make, you shall not make in the same proportions for yourselves; it shall be holy to you for the Lord* (Exodus 30:34-37).

These four compounds, stacte, onycha, galbanum, and frankincense, represent four qualities that need to be present in the incense of our prayers. Here is what they mean:

Stacte is a resinous sap that oozes through the bark of a type of tree that was a day's journey into Syria. In other words, it could only be obtained by walking into enemy territory. It *cost* the perfumer something to go and get the stacte. In the same way, it costs us something, and we have to go into enemy territory to gather the "drops," or Word of God, which bubble forth into prophecy. You have to store up the Word within your heart, and then it oozes forth in words of prophetic prayer. It's not an automatic-pilot sort of thing; you have to study to show yourself approved as a workman for God (see 2 Tim. 2:15).

Onycha came from the shell of a mollusk that lived in the Mediterranean Sea. Again, it took some effort to obtain it, because the perfumer had to walk so far. Then it had to be ground into a fine powder and further treated in order to give the incense its sweet odor when it was burned. In a similar way, our lives are to be broken before Him (see Ps. 51:17). The "fragrance" of our lives offered on the altar is well-pleasing to God. Prayer is made up of an equal portion of the Word and of brokenness in our lives.

Galbanum means "richness" or "fatness." Galbanum is a rich gum resin that holds the other ingredients together. Even though it is a bitter substance, it gives important tang to the fragrance, and it reminds us of the bitterness of sin. With the Spirit of Jesus dwelling in us, we possess his rich grace, which we exhibit through lives of faith and praise.

Frankincense is commonly known because it was one of the gifts brought by the Magi to the infant Jesus (see Matt. 2:11). In Old Testament times, it was known as *lavonah*, which means "white." In our prayers, we need the purity and "whiteness" of the righteousness that comes as God's gift to us, not because of our actions, but because of the sacrifice that Jesus accomplished.

Those are the requirements, the ingredients, which, in terms of our prayer lives, will cost us something and take some time to develop. Although some people like to "camp out" around one favorite ingredient or another (the Word, or the messages of brokenness, "fatness," or holiness), we need to have a balance of all four. Otherwise, our incense of prayer doesn't stick together right or "burn" with a pleasing fragrance to God.

Besides having the required ingredients blended together skillfully, the incense needs to be blended fresh every day. It cannot be made up in large batches ahead of time. It's the same in our daily prayer lives. You can't "bank" your prayers and expect them to work. We must depend upon Him constantly, continually, hourly. You need to burn that incense. Pray those prayers. Add fire—fervency and zeal—to these ingredients. He is worthy of perfect prayers offered up corporately by the Body of Christ around the globe, around the clock, and around the calendar.

A SWEET-SMELLING FRAGRANCE

You may know the name of Jackie Pullinger, a British woman who has lived for decades in Hong Kong, following whatever God tells her to do as she reaches out to people who do not know Him. Early in her time there, she met a man named Alie, who was studying to be a Buddhist priest until he was put in jail for a murder that he did not commit. (I heard her tell this story years ago.) Jackie would pray for him and go to see him often, on more than a weekly basis. One day, when she was praying for him in the jail, she could see that he was broken and that he felt hopeless. She put her hand up to the glass that separated them, and Alie put his hand up to the glass too. She told him, "I have people in England and the United States and South Africa who fast and pray every Wednesday, and I will ask them to fast and pray for you every Wednesday." After that, she did not see him for some time.

One day, the captain of the jail smelled a sweet fragrance in the place, and he could not figure out what it was. He followed the scented trail down the hallway of jail cells until it became strongest at Alie's cell. He went into the cell and demanded to know, "What is this sweet-smelling fragrance that I smell?" Alie smelled nothing. He went and he searched his clothing to try to find the source of this fragrance, but he could find nothing. The jailer left. Alie was now alone in the cell, and now he too could smell the sweet fragrance. What was this mysterious, wonderful odor? All of a sudden, a light bulb went on in Alie's mind, and he realized, "Ah! It is Wednesday! The day the people are fasting and praying for me!" He realized that he was smelling prayer! His jail cell was filled with the aroma of the prayers of the saints.

The next time Jackie visited, he told her what had happened. Eventually, as they continued to talk, his hardened heart broke open, and he accepted Jesus and was baptized in the Holy Spirit. Alie was saved by the prayers of the saints. And when his trial came, the judge released him without ever hearing the charges.

My question for you is, "Who is smelling your prayers?" Who are you lifting up in prayer on a regular basis? Worship, pray, and intercede as much as you can, because it is a sweet-smelling fragrance to the Lord, like burning incense in His nostrils.

Let the Prayer Storm Begin!

Now is the time for the Prayer Storm to begin. Our prayer is more than four components or qualities mixed equally together. It is more than Seven Effective Steps or a list of rules. It is not merely a systematic methodology. Prayer is communion with God, a relationship with your Father. Prayer is life.

Prayer is our destiny. It is our call as a New Testament priesthood of believers!

Let us be possessed by God and His purposes in this hour. Let us be possessed by the Spirit of grace and supplication for the purposes of prayer. May believers arise around the world who will intercede in their homes, prayer rooms, congregations, and ministries with hourly worship and prayer to give to the Lamb the rewards for His suffering. Let us restore and release the global Moravian lampstand for Jesus Christ's sake. Let God's prayer warriors arise, and let the Prayer Storm begin! Let the hour that changes the world begin!

> *Father, I present myself to You for the purpose of prayer. I join the host of others who are praying at this time. Come, Holy Spirit, and take possession of us all. Fill me with the Spirit of grace and supplication in Jesus' name and for the sake of His Kingdom. I volunteer freely in the day of Your power to be a watchman on the walls for such a time as this. Amen.*

Where He Leads Me

I can hear my Savior calling,
I can hear my Savior calling,
I can hear my Savior calling,
"Take thy cross and follow, follow Me."

(Refrain) *Where He leads me I will follow,*
Where He leads me I will follow,
Where He leads me I will follow;
I'll go with Him, with Him, all the way.

I'll go with Him through the garden,
I'll go with Him through the garden,
I'll go with Him through the garden,
I'll go with Him, with Him all the way.

I'll go with Him through the judgment,
I'll go with Him through the judgment,
I'll go with Him through the judgment,
I'll go with Him, with Him all the way.

He will give me grace and glory,
He will give me grace and glory,
He will give me grace and glory,
And go with me, with me all the way.[1]

Chapter 2

WALKING IN THE FOOTSTEPS OF JESUS

"You are a priest forever According to the order of Melchizedek."...He, because He continues forever, has an unchangeable priesthood. Therefore He is also able to save to the uttermost those who come to God through Him, since He always lives to make intercession for them (Hebrews 7:17,24-25 **NKJV**).

Jesus is our magnificent intercessor. He stood in the gap when He was crucified, and He stands in the gap to this day. He "always lives to make intercession," and He enables each one of us to participate with Him in that most effective expression of God's love—ceaseless intercessory prayer.

Have you ever thought about Jesus' earthly prayer life? His expressions of prayer are a model for us; in every way and on every level, they demonstrate for us the "how-to" of effective prayer. How often did He pray? Certainly He carried on an undercurrent of conversation with His Father while he went about His daily life. But He prayed all night before choosing the 12 disciples. Think about that a minute. "All night" means He prayed for eight or ten hours straight, outdoors, in the dark, on a mountain, alone. He didn't stop until He was sure He knew the Father's will. He missed a whole night's sleep. Jesus, the Son, who was so close to His Father, had to press in to His Father God all night long before he could be sure He was making the right decision: "It was at this time that He went off to the mountain to pray, and He spent the whole night in prayer to God. And when day came, He called His disciples to Him and chose twelve of them, whom He also named as apostles" (Luke 6:12-13).

Isn't that amazing? There was the Creator of the universe, Jesus, but He was walking in such total dependency on God the Father that He spent the entire night praying to Him. If only more of us would follow that example before choosing leaders, I think we might avoid a lot of mistakes and premature decisions. I think Jesus would have kept praying for two or three nights if that's what had been needed. But at the end of one solid night of praying, He knew which men to choose as his main disciples, so He went down the mountain to gather them together.

How did He pray? Do you think He closed His eyes and bowed His head and folded His hands? I don't think so. I think He raised His eyes and raised His head and raised his hands toward Heaven. I'm sure He prayed out loud, often, like this: "In the days of His flesh, He offered up both prayers and supplications with loud crying and tears to the One able to save Him from death, and He was heard because of His piety" (Heb. 5:7).

Now of course, there is a place for quiet, reflective prayer. But there is definitely a significant place for fervent, loud, emotional praying. In fact, in times of desperation or crisis, we can turn the volume up without worrying that somehow we are becoming less reverent or holy. Jesus did it, and so can we. Jesus prayed fervently, even with vehemence.

But vehemence was not the only emotion that He revealed when He prayed. Look at His emotional response to the tragic death of His friend Lazarus:

> *When Jesus saw* [Mary] *sobbing, and the Jews who came with her [also] sobbing, He was* **deeply moved in spirit and troubled. [He chafed in spirit and sighed and was disturbed.]** *And He said, "Where have you laid him?" They said to Him, "Lord, come and see." Jesus wept. The Jews said, "***See how [tenderly] He loved him!***" But some of them said, "Could not He Who opened a blind man's eyes have prevented this man from dying?" Now Jesus,* **again sighing repeatedly and deeply disquieted,** *approached the tomb. It was a cave (a hole in the rock), and a boulder lay against [the entrance to close] it* (John 11:33-38 AMP).

Obviously, Jesus wanted to demonstrate His lordship over death. But to do that, He could have simply marched up to the tomb and commanded Lazarus to come out with an "I told you so" attitude. Instead, He was *moved* by the situation. His emotions were stirred, deeply. Here were Lazarus' two unmarried sisters, Mary and Martha, who had been entirely dependent on their brother for their livelihood. The two sisters and their brother Lazarus were Jesus' special friends. He had stayed in their home as a guest; He had eaten meals with them; He had listened to them, and they had listened to Him. With them, He was at ease. They cared about each other. This man Lazarus was one of His closest personal friends, even though he wasn't one of His disciples. So when He saw Lazarus' sisters, Mary and Martha, torn with their grief, sobbing, His heart was torn with grief too.

The Bible says that He was "deeply moved." The Greek verb that we translate "deeply moved" is *embrimaomai*, which comes from the word *brimaomai,* or "to snort with anger." *Embrimaomai* means "to have indignation on, i.e., to blame, to sigh with chagrin [which implies being distressed],…to groan, to murmur against."[2] Jesus was grief-stricken, and He was upset. Death had robbed them of Lazarus. This was too much to bear! Jesus wept. He shed tears. He prayed from the depths of His heart with an outward expression that must have sounded like a snorting sigh or a muffled groan. He prayed to His Father. Jesus was praying out of His innermost being—out of the depths of His heart. He prayed with *compassion* intercession.

As he approached the tomb, the sorrow was like waves coming over Him, and He could no longer contain Himself. He sighed. His chest heaved. Tears streaked down His face. He was overwhelmed with a combination of loss and indignation at the enemy who had caused so much anguish for Him and for others. His very groans were a type of praying. He was in deep communication with the Father as He arrived directly in front of the opening of the tomb, which had been closed off with a large stone.

Then, Scripture tells us that, for the sake of those who were watching Him, who had already heard His sighs, He spoke a three-word prayer, "Lazarus, come forth!" Miracle of miracles, Lazarus did (see John 11:43-44).

Jesus had prayed out of His *function* as Messiah when he prayed all night about which men to choose as His disciples. Later, when He was facing His own death, He prayed out of His *desperation.* And in this case, He prayed out of *compassion.* He felt the inconsolable sorrow of Mary and Martha, and He was in deep emotional pain because His personal friend, Lazarus, had died.

As we follow in the footsteps of Jesus, we can pray as He prayed. We can pray out of our function, whatever we have been called to do. We can pray out of desperation, unashamedly and loudly. And we can pray out of compassion when we are moved to the depths emotionally. Jesus is our example all the way.

JESUS, AT THE RIGHT HAND OF THE FATHER

Another way we follow Jesus' example is by our confidence in our standing before the Father. We learn from John's first letter that Jesus is our Advocate before the Father, the One who stands before the Judge on our behalf: "If anyone sins, we have an Advocate with the Father, Jesus Christ the righteous" (1 John 2:1b).

It is significant that He is at the *right* hand of God. The right hand signifies authority and privilege. In that position, Jesus is as close to the Father as He can be. As He represents "cases" to the Judge, He is in a position to plead for mercy, and He has the authority to claim merciful judgments on behalf of those He represents. Have you ever noticed how many times this is portrayed throughout the Bible? Look at these verses:

> *Jesus replied. "But I say to all of you: In the future you will see the Son of Man sitting at the right hand of the Mighty One and coming on the clouds of heaven"* (Matthew 26:64b NIV).

> *So then, when the Lord Jesus had spoken to them, He was received up into heaven and sat down at the right hand of God* (Mark 16:19).

> *The Lord says to my Lord: "Sit at My right hand until I make Your enemies a footstool for Your feet"* (Psalm 110:1).

> *Which He brought about in Christ, when He raised Him from the dead and seated Him at His right hand in the heavenly places* (Ephesians 1:20).

Therefore if you have been raised up with Christ, keep seeking the things above, where Christ is, seated at the right hand of God (Colossians 3:1).

The Son is the radiance of God's glory and the exact representation of His being, sustaining all things by His powerful word. After He had provided purification for sins, He sat down at the right hand of the Majesty in Heaven (Hebrews 1:3 NIV).

The point of what we are saying is this: We do have such a high priest, who sat down at the right hand of the throne of the Majesty in heaven, and who serves in the sanctuary, the true tabernacle set up by the Lord, not by man....He entered the Most Holy Place once for all by His own blood, having obtained eternal redemption....For this reason Christ is the mediator of a new covenant, that those who are called may receive the promised eternal inheritance—now that He has died as a ransom to set them free from the sins committed under the first covenant (Hebrews 8:1-2; 9:12,15 NIV).

So we see that Jesus was not only an intercessor when He was walking on the earth over two thousand years ago. He also ascended to sit at the Father's right hand, which means that He is in the ultimate intercessory position. Thank God He is there! Thank God there is an intercessor, a go-between, between us (in our unrighteousness) and judgment that the Father would otherwise mete out to us. We cannot earn His favor. We need mercy, because there is nothing else we can do to avoid a guilty verdict. Jesus interceded while He was walking with us on earth, He paid the ultimate price when He put Himself between our sin and God's righteous condemnation, and He still intercedes for us from his position at the right hand of God.

JESUS' ONGOING ACTIVITY IN HEAVEN

In Heaven, Jesus' ongoing activity is to mediate the New Covenant, drawing to Himself those who so desperately need the saving power of His blood. Speaking about the blood of the Lamb Jesus, the great preacher Charles Spurgeon said, "Many keys fit many locks, but the master key is the blood and the name of Him that died, and rose again, and ever lives in heaven to save unto the uttermost. The blood of Christ is that which unlocks the treasury of heaven."[3] Spurgeon's phrase, "to save unto the uttermost" comes from the words of Hebrews 7:25, which reads like this in two different English versions:

Wherefore He is able also to save them to the uttermost that come unto God by Him, seeing He ever liveth to make intercession for them (Hebrews 7:25 KJV).

Therefore He is able also to save to the uttermost (completely, perfectly, finally, and for all time and eternity) those who come to God through Him, since He is always living to make petition to God and intercede with Him and intervene for them (Hebrews 7:25 AMP).

The blood of Jesus doesn't speak only in the past, historical tense, but it is still alive and effective today, speaking (interceding)—"Mercy. Mercy. Mercy." It is able to save to the uttermost, past, present, and future. Jesus' blood speaks because Jesus Himself speaks on our behalf, continually: "...and to Jesus, the mediator of a new covenant, and to the sprinkled blood, which speaks better than the blood of Abel" (Heb. 12:24). The words that Jesus speaks do not return to Him void (see Isa. 55:10-11). His prayers are perfect, because He is perfect. We can depend utterly on His prayers for mercy. We can bank on Him.

We can also pray with Him. He is our model, and He provides the words for us to use. We can pray the Word, and it will not return to *us* void. We can pray in the Spirit when, otherwise, we would be at the end of ourselves, and Jesus' Spirit will pray through us in just the right way. Sometimes I am at a loss. I do not know what to pray. But I know that I can just turn myself and my situation over to my Savior, Jesus, and (doing as Peter said) cast all my cares upon Him, because He cares for me (see 1 Pet. 5:7). I say, "Jesus, You have to take care of it. Intercede for me. I come into agreement with whatever the Father wants to do. I yield myself to You."

JESUS CHRIST, OUR PRIESTLY MODEL

Intercession reached its fullest and most profound expression when the sins of the whole world were laid upon Jesus. It is little wonder that the Bible calls this a mystery. It is difficult to comprehend, and it is almost unthinkable that the God of the universe would make such a provision for human beings. Somehow, in the wisdom of God, Jesus was made able to identify fully with us, carrying the totality of our human condition. Then, with our sins laid upon Him, as the Old Testament priests used to lay sins upon a scapegoat, He carried our sins away forever. He didn't just pick up our burden; He did something with it. He carried away our sins, which would have condemned us. "As far as the east is from the west, so far has He removed our transgressions from us" (Ps. 103:12).

The word for "carry" or "bear" in Hebrew is *nasa*, and it means "to lift up, bear away, removed to a distance."[4] We see this word in the 53rd chapter of Isaiah:

> ...*My Servant, will justify the many, as He will bear their iniquities....Because He poured out Himself to death, and was numbered with the transgressors; yet He Himself bore*

the sin of many, and interceded for the transgressors (Isaiah 53:11-12).

We, as His Body, can enter into this form of intercession. We are just riding along with Him, of course, because we can't redeem ourselves, and we need His gift of redemption all the way, but there is something about our sharing in His sufferings on behalf of His Body, the Church. Somehow we can help "fill up" the rest of what is needed. As I quoted in the previous chapter, Colossians 1:24 tells us, "Now I rejoice in my sufferings for your sake, and in my flesh I do my share on behalf of His body, which is the church, in filling up what is lacking in Christ's afflictions." On behalf of others, even those who appear to be complete rascals, we can intercede, pleading for mercy and forgiveness of sin. We can pick up their burdens.

In intercessors' language, we can have a "prayer burden." We pick up the burden in order to do something with it—to lift it up and remove it, to carry it far away. Don't be an intercessor who comes under a burden from the Lord and who stays there too long, trying to hold up under it. Don't keep the burden! Pray until it's gone. Take the further step and cast it away, as Jesus did and does. There is such a thing as burden-bearing, but it's not supposed to be a perpetual state of being. The point is to lift that burden off someone and to transport it a distance so that it will not return. You can pick up a spirit of depression over a family, and you can cast it away. This is a joyful assignment, not a heavy one!

This is part of the priestly function of Jesus and, by extension, those of us who are the "priesthood of all believers" (see 1 Pet. 2). This priestly role of bearing other's burdens away was prophesied by Isaiah, centuries before it became a reality through the birth, life, and death of Jesus:

All of us like sheep have gone astray, each of us has turned to his own way; but the Lord has caused the iniquity of us all to fall on Him....Therefore, I will allot Him a portion with the great, and He will divide the booty with the strong; because He poured out Himself to death, and was numbered with the transgressors; yet He Himself bore the sin of many, and interceded for the transgressors (Isaiah 53:6,12).

Jesus Christ became our model, humbling Himself through extreme means:

[He] *emptied Himself, taking the form of a bond-servant, and being made in the likeness of men. Being found in appearance as a man, He humbled Himself by becoming obedient to the point of death, even death on a cross* (Philippians 2:7-8).

Jesus' humble obedience resulted in exaltation from the Father. In this case, it is not "what goes up must come down," but it is "what comes down will go up." God has an upside-down Kingdom, and He loves it when we follow in the footsteps of Jesus and humble ourselves! This allows Him to receive the glory when favor or exaltation comes. Another pertinent Scripture shows us how He took on all of the sins of mankind so that we might "become the righteousness of God" in Him: "He made Him who knew no sin to be sin on our behalf, so that we might become the righteousness of God in Him" (2 Cor. 5:21).

I have been praying about this verse for 30 years, over and over, asking for a greater revelation of it. It's profound, and I'm still asking. I understand it to a degree, but there are depths in there that I still don't grasp. The verse doesn't say that He took our sins right there. It says, "He who knew no sin *became* sin." He became, somehow, all the sin of the entire world, past, present, and future. He did it so that we could—in some mysterious way—"become the righteousness of God in Him."

Jesus, even when He was in His death throes on the cross, said, "Father, forgive them, for they do not know what they are doing" (Luke 23:34). He was an intercessor right through the most difficult time of all, even when you would think the order of the day would be vengeance with a capital V. From the cross, with His blood running down His forehead and into his mouth, Jesus was still interceding. Instead of calling down fire from Heaven on those who had accused Him falsely and mocked Him and practically pulled Him limb from limb, Jesus remained so aware of the Father's loving purpose that He asked His Father to forgive everyone for everything.

Jesus shows us one of the keys for intercession—knowing the love of the Father. We need to become intimately aware of the Father's heart and to feel secure in His love. Then we can pray as Jesus prayed. He is so much our model and guide that He will help us toward greater and greater security in His love, even as we indicate to Him our desire to live and pray as He did and does.

To pray like Jesus, you need to have an unoffended heart. Then you too can say, "Father, forgive them, for they know not what they do." You can stand in the gap for your generation, for your family. I call it "ambassadorial intercession," because you're acting as an ambassador for Christ. You are representing people before Him and asking Him to forgive them.

OUR ROLE AS PRIESTLY BURDEN-BEARERS

I want to take you back to this idea of intercession as burden-bearing. In the Greek, the idea of burden-bearing is covered by the word *bastazo*. According to *Strong's Concordance*, *bastazo* is a verb that means, "to take up with the hands," "to take up in order to carry or bear," "to bear what is burdensome," "to bear, to carry," "to carry on one's person," "to sustain, i.e. uphold, support," "to bear away, carry off."[5] *Bastazo* is the word that is used in Romans 15:1-3 and Galatians 6:2:

> *Now we who are strong ought to bear the weaknesses of those without strength and not just please ourselves. Each of us is to please his neighbor for his good, to his edification. For even Christ did not please Himself; but as it is written, "The reproaches of those who reproached You fell on Me"* (Romans 15:1-3).

> *Bear one another's burdens, and so fulfill the law of Christ* (Galatians 6:2 NKJV).

Intercessors "bear off" or carry off the burdens of others. This is not the same as "bearing up" under a load, because when you pray, you offload it, with God's help, as quickly as you can.

In the last portion of the Romans passage above, we read, "the reproaches of those who reproached You fell on Me." What does that mean? Reproaches are criticisms, verbalized. It means that Jesus bears off the burden of critical speech just as completely as other kinds of burdens. Because of Him, so do we. We lift up those heavy words and shoulder them, carrying them to Jesus in prayer and forgiveness.

This is what He did for us, and it's what He wants us to do for each other. He wants us to usher each other along, carrying each other's burdens in prayer to Him. This can be emotionally difficult. It involves weeping with those who weep sometimes (see Rom. 12:15). It involves being willing to help carry burdens for a long time, walking alongside people who are not easy to love.

Another Greek word is used to portray this kind of burden-bearing: *anechomai*. In the King James Version, it is translated with the words "bear with," "endure," "forbear," and even "suffer." In the *New American Standard Bible*, we find it translated as "bear," "bearing," "endure," "showing tolerance," and "tolerate." The word can also imply "to stake up," like staking up a weak plant, supporting something so that when the winds of adversity blow, a weak person has extra support.[6] Here is the word as it's translated in the following Scriptures:

> *So, as those who have been chosen of God, holy and beloved, put on a heart of compassion, kindness, humility, gentleness and patience; bearing with one another, and forgiving each other, whoever has a complaint against anyone; just as the Lord forgave you, so also should you* (Colossians 3:12-13).

> *Therefore I...implore you to walk in a manner worthy of the calling with which you have been called, with all humility and gentleness, with patience, showing tolerance for one another in love* (Ephesians 4:1-2).

All of this is the work of Christ. We are His ambassadors, and we are merely imitating Him and operating out of the grace that He supplies when we sympathize and empathize with other people and help them carry their loads. It's part of our role as priestly burden-bearers, because this is the work of the Kingdom:

> *This was to fulfill what was spoken through Isaiah the prophet: "He Himself took our infirmities and carried away our diseases"* (Matthew 8:17).

> *For we do not have a high priest who cannot sympathize with our weaknesses, but One who has been tempted in all things as we are, yet without sin* (Hebrews 4:15).

Now all these things are from God, who reconciled us to Himself through Christ and gave us the ministry of reconciliation, namely, that God was in Christ reconciling the world to Himself, not counting their trespasses against them, and He has committed to us the word of reconciliation. Therefore, we are ambassadors for Christ, as though God were making an appeal through us; we beg you on behalf of Christ, be reconciled to God. He made Him who knew no sin to be sin on our behalf, so that we might become the righteousness of God in Him. And working together with Him, we also urge you not to receive the grace of God in vain (2 Corinthians 5:18–6:1).

INVITED TO PARTICIPATE IN THE WORK OF CHRIST

So we, as prayer ambassadors, have been invited to participate in the work of Christ Jesus, sharing in His joys and in His sorrows. We are privileged to call His loving attention to the needs of others. God has "raised us up with Him, and seated us with Him in the heavenly places in Christ Jesus" (Eph. 2:6). He has called those of us who bear His name "the priests of the Lord" and "ministers of our God" (Isa. 61:6).

Have you appropriated the truth of that statement yet? I have been called to be a priest of the Lord and a minister of God, and *you* have been called to be a priest of the Lord and a minister of God. We will be spoken of as priests and ministers. We sit with Him at the right hand of the Father. This is manifestly true. The truth of it is starting to be worked out in our lives as actual experience.

From our position with Him in Heaven, it is our great joy and honor to intercede for others, to bridge the gap that separates them from His provision. Just as Jesus is our tireless Intercessor, so we keep the fires of intercession burning day and night. Because we "have been raised up with Christ," we "keep seeking the things above, where Christ is, seated at the right hand of God" (Col. 3:1).

It is *from* our position with Him—not from a position far beneath the clouds—that we seek His intervention. We pray from up here to down there. We're not praying up through this temporary present darkness, blindly groping our way, hoping against hope that at least a few of our efforts will prevail. No, we start out seated on high. We're praying *down* through the darkness, from the throne room!

Through our prayers, especially as they are joined to the prayers of other like-minded and "like-hearted" servants of the King, we have the authority to call forth prayer-targets. Our intercession releases His glory light to flash forth like lightening and helps to aim it at the desired objective. As we noted in Chapter 1, "He covers His hands with the lightening and commands it to strike the mark" (Job 36:32).

We are seated with Him; therefore, we can share His perspective. With His eyes, we can see. Our worship-filled hearts fasten themselves to Him. He is the object of our desire. Our prayers flow from hearts that have been captured by His.

As our High Priest forever (see Heb. 7:24), Jesus nevertheless remains the Son of Man. His intercession comes from his heart as the Son of Man. Here is what Wesley Duewel says about this:

> As enthroned Son of Man, what does Jesus live to do? Does He live to welcome the saints to heaven at their death? I am sure He welcomes them, but the Bible does not say so. Does He live to grant interviews to saints and angels? He most probably does this, but the Bible does not say so. Does He live to enjoy heaven's

music? I am sure He thrills to do it. He created us to be able to enjoy music along with Him, but there is something more important than listening to music. Does He live to reign? Most certainly He does—and He will reign for ever and ever.

The Bible emphasizes one role of Jesus today above all others—He is *Priest* forever (Heb. 5:6; 6:20; 7:17,21). His priesthood is permanent (7:24) because He always lives to intercede (v. 25). His sovereign throne is a throne of grace, both because of His atonement and because He ever lives to intercede for us. His is a priestly throne (8:1).

Romans 8:34 associates two facts: Christ at the right hand of God, and Christ interceding for us. What does this intercession for us imply? Many commentators feel that His very presence seated on the throne of heaven is sufficient in itself as a glorious intercession. They doubt that He is actually praying. They feel that He does not need to make any requests of the Father; His sitting on the throne is all the request necessary.

But Jesus is the same yesterday, today, and forever (Heb. 13:8). While on earth, He loved us, yearned for us, and prayed for us (John 17). He prayed for Peter personally (Luke 22:32). As Son of Man, He is as intensely concerned about and interested in each one of us as He ever was. He is still as sympathetic as He ever was (Heb. 4:15). The Greek word used here, *sympatheō*, means "to suffer with." The whole argument of Hebrews 4:15-16 is that we are to come to the throne of grace (where Jesus is interceding) with confidence because He does sympathize and suffer with our pain. He is touched and moved by our need and feels its pain. He feels for us as infinitely as He ever did. His throne of intercession for us is a throne of feeling intercession.[7]

We cannot add to what Jesus has done, but modeling what He did, through the power of His Spirit in us, we have the burdens and weaknesses of others placed upon us for intercessory purposes. We carry them to the throne, allowing the Holy Spirit to appropriate the benefits of the cross, acknowledging and receiving the grace of our Lord and the power of His shed blood as all-sufficient for every possible need. His throne is a "throne of feeling intercession," and we stand with Him, willing and eager to intercede through Him.

Lord, I rejoice to know that Jesus Christ is our magnificent intercessor and High Priest and that He is our mediator and most excellent advocate. I draw near to Your glorious throne of grace to receive help and mercy. I draw near to Your heart. Grant me Your heart and Your grace for this deepening work of identification in intercession. Make me an ambassador. Open my eyes to see the needs and grant me Your broken heart. Help me to lay down my life as I agree to help carry people's burdens to You. As one of the ones You have called to co-labor with You in your priestly ministry, I want to volunteer myself freely to offer the incense of prayer, praise, thanksgiving, and intercession on behalf of others. Along with Your other servants, I want to enlist as a Prayer Warrior in Your holy name. Here I stand, Lord. I want to follow in Your footsteps! For Your Kingdom and Your glory's sake, amen.

Part II

Power for a Prayer Storm

Breathe on Me, Breath of God

Breathe on me, breath of God,
Fill me with life anew,
That I may love what Thou dost love,
And do what Thou wouldst do.

Breathe on me, breath of God,
Until my heart is pure,
Until with Thee I will one will,
To do and to endure.

Breathe on me, breath of God,
Blend all my soul with Thine,
Until this earthly part of me
Glows with Thy fire divine.

Breathe on me, breath of God,
So shall I never die,
But live with Thee the perfect life
Of Thine eternity.[1]

Chapter 3

SPIRIT-EMPOWERED PRAYER STORM

"I have heard you," replied Jeremiah the prophet. "I will certainly pray to the Lord your God as you have requested; I will tell you everything the Lord says and will keep nothing back from you" (Jeremiah 42:4 NIV).

For this chapter, I have chosen to use the term, *Spirit-empowered prayer,* although I have presented similar biblical overviews of prayer under different headings such as *prophetic intercession* or *revelatory prayer.* It seems that the idea of *Spirit-empowered prayer* is easier to grasp than some of the other terms that I and others have often used. What do I mean by the term? It's straightforward enough; I'm talking about prayer that is directed and led by the Holy Spirit.

This kind of prayer is like being in a great waltz in which you let the Holy Spirit take the lead. He not only leads you, but He also propels you. He not only nudges you this way and that, but He sometimes keeps you dancing all night! Spirit-empowered prayer is like getting a booster to your prayer rocket. Just like He did on the day of Pentecost in the Book of Acts (see Acts 2), the Holy Spirit comes upon you and rises up within you. He gives you a burst of power, energy, and insight that you did not possess previously.

Paul wrote these words to the church in Rome: "All who are being led by the Spirit of God, these are the sons of God"

(Rom. 8:14). As God's children, naturally we want to be led by Him. We want to keep up with Him. We want to walk in His footsteps. It doesn't take us very long before we realize that we cannot accomplish this without the power of the Holy Spirit. In our humanity, we do not come equipped with the kind of power—the impetus, the insight, the influence—that is required to accomplish God's work. We need to be filled with divine power.

Prophetic intercession is the ability to receive an immediate prayer request from God and to pray about it in a divinely anointed utterance. *Prophetic prayer* is waiting before God in order to "hear" or receive God's burden (which means God's concern, warning, conditions, vision, promise, or word) and then responding back to the Lord and to the people, with appropriate actions. The types of prayer, whatever you want to call them (prophetic intercession, prophetic prayer, revelatory prayer), and the appropriate actions (responses and "techniques" of prayer) are all included under Spirit-empowered prayer.

THE POWER OF PROPHETIC INTERCESSION

In my book, *The Prophetic Intercessor,* I developed the biblical basis for prophetic intercession with thorough teaching and numerous examples from Church history and my own life's journey. But for this one chapter, let me simply give you an overview of this subject that is so dear to my heart.

In the Scripture I quoted at the beginning of this chapter, Jeremiah the prophet agreed to pray on behalf of the people, and he agreed to listen to God for them. This is what prophets do—they can "hear" God (whether or not they hear an audible voice), and they are able to tell people what God has said. In this instance, Jeremiah was combining his prophetic role with the priestly role of intercession.

In prophetic intercession, the roles of priest and prophet are brought together. Not all prophets are intercessors, and not all priests are prophets. But when these two come together, it can be powerful! In authentic prophetic intercession, the graces and burdens of the prophet and the priest are united. The priest pleads the needs of the people to the Lord. The prophet pleads the interests of God before the people. The prophetic intercessor does both.

Prophetic Intercession Pleads the Promises

As an intercessor rises in worship, he or she becomes securely seated with Christ Jesus in the heavenly places. As a result, the intercessor receives a revelation of His heart. With that revelation, the intercessor is able to pray *with* God instead of merely *to* Him from his or her own limited perspective and passion. The intercessor becomes prophetic. The words of intercession become reiterations of God's Word. They match up with the will of God. The prophetic intercessor pleads the promises of God.

This makes an amazing difference in the effectiveness of prayer. When God enables you to pray like this, your prayers can be based not only on the covenant promises of God that He has made to His people and that are recorded in the Bible, but also on the rest of the unfulfilled promises that He has made to His people throughout history.

You are like John the Beloved, leaning your head upon the chest of the Messiah. You are hearing the very heartbeat of Heaven, and that heartbeat begins to resonate within you. Your words of prayer arise from your heart, which is filled with His

Spirit, and that means that they are guaranteed to be in agreement with God—which makes them highly effective.

The words of this kind of revelatory prayer pave the way for the realization of as-yet-unfulfilled prophetic promises. In this kind of prophetic intercession, the Spirit of God pleads through you as a believer. Your prayer "targets" are painted with greater accuracy. Not only does the Spirit urge you to pray prayers that have been prayed for centuries ("Come, Lord Jesus"), but He also enables you, as a Spirit-filled intercessor, to "pick up on" immediate prayer requests that are on the heart of God ("Lord, anoint the preaching of Your Word this evening"). The Holy Spirit nudges you to pray for particular things in particular ways so that He can intervene. You are given revelation for situations about which you have very little knowledge in the natural. Whether your prayer requests are small or large, you know you can be confident that they will be bringing forth His will on the earth as it is willed in Heaven.

THE ANNA COMPANY

God is looking for a particular kind of people. He is looking for Holy Ghost *pushers*. He's looking for people who He can put on assignment, people who will press and push in their praying until something happens. He wants these people to join hands and take their places as watchmen on the wall for His sake, for the sake of His coming Kingdom. He is looking for Annas and Simeons who will pray relentlessly:

> *Now there was a man in Jerusalem called Simeon, who was righteous and devout. He was waiting for the consolation of Israel, and the Holy Spirit was upon him. It had been revealed to him by the Holy Spirit that he would not die before he had seen the Lord's Christ (Luke 2:25-26 NIV).*

*And there was a prophetess, Anna the daughter of
Phanuel, of the tribe of Asher She was advanced in years
and had lived with her husband seven years after her marriage, and then as a widow to the age of eighty-four. She
never left the temple, serving night and day with fastings
and prayers. At that very moment she came up and began
giving thanks to God, and continued to speak of Him to all
those who were looking for the redemption of Jerusalem*
(Luke 2:36-38).

Anna's assignment was prayer, specifically prayer that
would prepare the way for the coming of the Messiah. Her story
helps us understand our own prayer assignments. She stayed
there in the temple, fasting and praying, day after day, week
after week, year after year. She worshiped and prayed through
the promises of God. God had promised to send a Savior. She
was waiting for Him, not passively or with resignation, but
actively, with prayer.

I believe that, just as God had Anna and Simeon before
the first coming of Jesus, so it will be before His Second Coming. I believe that there will be consecrated, gifted, prophetic
intercessors who will lay hold of the purposes of God. May it
happen in this generation! The Lord wants to raise up an Anna
company in our day, intercessors who will pave the way for the
second coming of the Lord. He is looking for new recruits; the
Holy Spirit is sending out invitations. Have you responded yet?

Now when I say "Anna company," I don't mean that this
assignment is for women only. It's true that many of the greatest intercessors of our time have been women. They have a natural sensitivity of spirit and a passion for the things of God.
They are ready to yield their hearts to Him to plead his cause.
But the Anna company is made up of both men and women,
young as well as old. The only qualification that you need, in

order to belong, is an ever-growing conviction of the end-time purposes of God and a desire to pray through God's promises until you see them fulfilled.

The members of the Anna company know how the burden of prophetic intercession begins as a small flame and soon consumes everything around it as revelation increases. They know how the burden grows throughout its "gestation period," and they learn how to travail and how to push in prayer in order to bring God's purposes to birth. All prophetic intercession carries with it the struggle of birth. The hearts of prophetic intercessors becomes wombs in which God's prophetic purposes can grow until it's time for them to come forth. Arise, people of God, and put off your slumber! Let us become steadfast and single-minded, like Anna, more than 2,000 years ago. When we see Him, let us cry out, "Behold the Christ!"

PROPHETIC INTERCESSION = CONSPIRING

The word *conspire* means "to breathe together." When God created man from the dust of the earth, He breathed into his nostrils the breath of life, and man became a living being (see Gen. 2:7). This Hebrew word that we translate "breathed" can mean breathing violently, such as when the violent, rushing wind filled the upper room on the day of Pentecost.[2]

The prophetic intercessor *conspires* with God that His glory will be seen, felt, and known in the earth. Prophetic intercession is our conspiring (breathing together) with God, breathing violently into situations through prayer in order to bring forth life. Here's an example from my own life.

Some years back, I was in Germany. In the middle of the night, I took a train from Heidelberg to Rosenheim, which is in the part of southern Germany that is known as Bavaria. It was a six-hour trip. All night long, as I attempted to rest on the train, I kept hearing the gentle, consistent voice of the Holy Spirit. After a while, it was as if I were breathing these words with Him. The same phrase rumbled over and over within my mind and heart as the train rumbled its way across Germany: "Where are my Daniels? Where are my Esthers? Where are my Deborahs? Where are my Josephs?" I heard it over and over. "Where are my Daniels? Where are my Esthers? Where are my Deborahs? Where are my Josephs?"

I knew He was talking to me as an individual intercessor, but I also felt He was imparting to me a burden to raise up a band of people who would volunteer themselves for the task of prayer. It was as if the Spirit and I were *con-spiring*, breathing together, for the purpose of bringing life into something that was in the heart of God. Where *are* His Daniels, Esthers, Deborahs, and Josephs? Are you one of them? Have you been positioned "for such a time as this"? (See Esther 4:14.) Have you been brought forth for this prophetic intercessory task? Will you be one of the answers to His persistent plea?

Many years ago, I saw a vision of "velvet warriors" moving forward on their knees. It was the army of the Lord, but they were coming so much more slowly than I would have anticipated. When I saw them come to the top of a hill, I could see why—they were marching on their knees. Then the Spirit described them to me as velvet warriors. This indicated that they were part of an arising generation that knew that its strength was on bended knee.

That army is still assembling, and many vacancies still exist in it; you can still sign up. It's not too late to answer the call. You can volunteer for on-the-job training and be commissioned as one of God's servant warriors. I think I can hear drumbeats in the background. I think I can hear another sound calling forth watchmen to mount their walls. Who will answer these calls? Who will blend their heartbeat and their heart's cry with His?

FORMS OF SPIRIT-EMPOWERED PRAYER

Spirit-empowered prayer can take many forms, as the Spirit blows wherever He wishes. But two forms of Spirit-inspired prayer, which are completely biblical and completely under the oversight of the Holy Spirit, are praying in the Spirit through the gift of tongues and praying in the Spirit through intense, fervent prayer (prayer that is so intense it is like the "travail" of natural childbirth). Tongues and travail. I want to spend the rest of the chapter on these two forms of prayer.

The Gift of Tongues

The gift of tongues—what a wonderful dimension of prayer! I love to pray in tongues. I probably pray in this way more than I do in any other way. Of course, I pray in English all the time. I read the Word of God, and then I pray it. But one of the keys that opens revelation for me is praying in tongues, first in a devotional way and then, as the Spirit arises within me, in the intercessory dimension of the gift. I'm not saying that it's the only way to pray, because it's not; it's just a way. There are many forms of Spirit-led, Spirit-empowered prayer. But praying with the gift of tongues is one of the primary ones.

When you pray in the Spirit, your spirit is communicating directly with God. It's a straight shot. You can pray in your prayer language as much as you want to, using it to raise yourself up to new levels in praise, worship, and intercession. The Word tells us: "For anyone who speaks in a tongue does not speak to men but to God. Indeed, no one understands him; he utters mysteries with his spirit" (1 Cor. 14:2 NIV).

When you pray privately in this way, whether quietly or loudly, sitting at your desk, standing at the kitchen sink, or driving your car, you are edifying and building yourself up in the Lord, uttering far more expressive praises to Him than you could think up on your own.

But you can also use this spiritual gift to intercede. You can bring a concern, care, or burden before the Lord and yield it to Him with words in your prayer language. In this way, the Holy Spirit intercedes through your spirit:

> *The Spirit helps us in our weakness. We do not know what we ought to pray for, but the Spirit Himself intercedes for us with groans that words cannot express. And He who searches our hearts knows the mind of the Spirit, because the Spirit intercedes for the saints in accordance with God's will* (Romans 8:26-28 NIV).

> *For if I pray in an [unknown] tongue, my spirit [by the Holy Spirit within me] prays, but my mind is unproductive [it bears no fruit and helps nobody]* (1 Corinthians 14:14 AMP).

Since none of us always knows how or what to pray in a given situation, bringing your prayer before the Lord by praying in the Spirit enables the Holy Spirit, your Helper, to pray within the Lord's will. Using a prayer language is a way of being dependent upon God, because you cannot duplicate it or invent it on your own. Sometimes people might act proud of it, as in "I have something better than you do," but needless to say, all that reveals is a character weakness in the speaker, not a flaw in the gift itself.

Years ago, when I did not yet exercise the gift of tongues, I thought I didn't need it. I said, "God gives that to those who need it, and I don't need it." As the next few months went by, the Lord convinced me that the first part of my statement was totally correct. God does give the gift to those who need it. But the second part of my statement was not correct, because I did need it! I had come up against some circumstances in my life that I could not solve. I wasn't trained enough. I wasn't knowledgeable enough. I wasn't experienced enough. I didn't seem to have enough prayer power on my own, so I yielded to the Holy Spirit. I now had a new revelation: God gives the gift to those who need it. And, guess what, that includes me. That was humbling.

Even though praying in the Spirit sounds nonsensical to your ear (because you really don't know what you're saying), your prayer language has definite meaning. It doesn't matter whether or not you understand it, because God does, and He is the One you are praying to. He who inspired it also comprehends it. First Corinthians 14:10 explains that "undoubtedly there are all sorts of languages in the world, yet none of them is without meaning" (NIV).

Use this gift often, because it will edify your spirit. You will be built up and strengthened, encouraged and reinvigorated for your intercessory warfare task. We read again in the 14th chapter of First Corinthians: "One who speaks in a tongue edifies himself" (1 Cor. 14:4a). In the Book of Jude, we read, "But you, dear friends, build yourselves up in your most holy faith and pray in the Holy Spirit" (Jude 20 NIV). So if you want to be in the Spirit and stay in the Spirit—pray in the Spirit!

Praying in the Spirit has the full authority of Heaven behind it! There is no way you could know in the natural when satan and his demonic forces are about to launch an attack, but the Holy Spirit will prompt you at the strategic, opportune time and will keep you on the alert. And because you know that "the effective prayer of a righteous man can accomplish much" (James 5:16b), you can be sure that you will prevail. You just prayed prayers that were inspired by the Spirit. And who is more righteous than the Holy Spirit?

You can pray both ways, in the Spirit and with your mind. That's what Paul did: "...I will pray with the spirit and I will pray with the mind also; I will sing with the spirit and I will sing with the mind also" (1 Cor. 14:15). Like Paul, you can pray in the Spirit to regain territory from the demonic kingdom, and you can express your prayers with unfailing faith and unwavering joy, praise, and worship. This prayer and praise weapon is powerful, and it's always on target. Praying in the Spirit is God's anti-ballistic missile, and it hits the mark every time!

Paul further instructed us about the gift of tongues:

> *Now concerning spiritual gifts, brethren, I would not have you ignorant....Now there are diversities of gifts, but the same Spirit. And there are differences of administrations, but the same Lord. And there are diversities of operations, but it is the same God which worketh all in all. But the manifestation of the Spirit is given to every man to profit withal....Now ye are the body of Christ, and members in particular. And God hath set some in the church, first apostles, secondarily prophets, thirdly teachers, after that miracles, then gifts of healings, helps, governments, diversities of tongues* (1 Corinthians 12:1,4-7,27-28 KJV).

He was saying, obviously, that there are different kinds of tongues. They sound different—really different—from each other. In that passage, the word translated "diversities" is *genos* in the Greek, and it refers to a collection of different things that belong to the same group or family, "kin" or "offspring."[3] In other words, diversities of tongues are all heavenly utterances that are as different as the members of a family or group can be, but they related to one another by the same Spirit.

As you know, the Holy Spirit loves diversity. If you have ever traveled widely, you will know what I mean. Not only is God's creation vast and filled with infinite variety, but human cultures and languages are too. I have traveled in well over 40 different nations on all of the continents, and I have heard some very strange dialects. Some languages sound like baby talk or just noise to my ear. But they are all languages, and they all have meaning. So if you hear other people speaking in prayer languages that don't sound very sophisticated to you—that's OK. Even in one person's range of experience with this gift, we see diversity.

This may be a bit of a review, but here are some diverse applications from the Bible for the gift of tongues:

- Tongues at the filling of the Holy Spirit (See Acts 2:1-4; 10:44-46; Mark 16:17.)

- Tongues for interpretation (See 1 Corinthians 12:7-10; Isaiah 28:11.)

- Tongues of edification (See Jude 20; 1 Corinthians 14:4.)

- Tongues as a sign to the unbeliever (See 1 Corinthians 14:22.)

- Tongues of intercession (See Romans 8:26. The word *groanings* in this verse can be translated as "inarticulate speech," and it refers to speech that does not originate in the intellect or with the understanding, speech that is not related to race or nationality. Inarticulate speech includes, but is not limited to, "other tongues.")[4]

- Tongues of warfare (Sometimes the Holy Spirit goes on the offensive. He battles through us. Sometimes He couples together the gift of tongues with the gift of faith or the gift of discerning of spirits. You will feel a rising up inside and a push or an urge to launch out against demonic forces. You attack the powers of darkness, taking authority over satan and rejecting his plans, and you do it by the power of the Holy Spirit who dwells within you. This is your tongue of intercession engaged in warfare, bringing deliverance, healing, and liberty.)

The Prayer of Groaning and Travail

Let's examine more in depth the Scripture I cited above under "tongues of intercession." Before long, most committed intercessors have the experience described in Romans 8:26-27, the experience of the Holy Spirit groaning and wrestling through their prayers. Here are two translations of these two verses:

In the same way the Spirit also helps our weakness; for we do not know how to pray as we should, but the Spirit Himself intercedes for us with groanings too deep for words; and He who searches the hearts knows what the mind of the Spirit is, because He intercedes for the saints according to the will of God (Romans 8:26-27).

So too the [Holy] Spirit comes to our aid and bears us up in our weakness; for we do not know what prayer to offer nor how to offer it worthily as we ought, but the Spirit Himself goes to meet our supplication and pleads in our behalf with unspeakable yearnings and groanings too deep for utterance. And He Who searches the hearts of men knows what is in the mind of the [Holy] Spirit [what His intent is], because the Spirit intercedes and pleads [before God] in behalf of the saints according to and in harmony with God's will (Romans 8:26-27 AMP).

Many times we call this kind of praying "travail," because it is so much like natural childbirth. It is the will of God to give birth to His purposes, but that process of birthing is not instantaneous or painless. It can be quite a struggle. Words alone can't accomplish it. The Holy Spirit in us moves beyond words to sighs, groans, and inarticulate longings. We move with our prayers. We may stand up and reach up to God, then pace, then fall to the floor, even writhing as we yearn for the relief of the longed-for "birth." It's work. It's very much like labor, purposeful and intense. In the heat of the effort, we no longer worry about maintaining our dignity.

This kind of praying is fervent. It is hot. (The word *fervent* comes from the Latin word for "to boil; hot.")[5] In this kind of intercession, we see God's intense desire to create an opening through which He can bring new life, change, growth, or fruit. Elijah modeled it for us:

Elijah was a man with a nature like ours, and he prayed earnestly that it would not rain, and it did not rain on the earth for three years and six months. Then he prayed again, and the sky poured rain and the earth produced its fruit (James 5:17-18).

Prayer that involves groaning and panting under the power of the Holy Spirit, like a woman in childbirth, can also be compared to the heat of a conflict on a battlefield. Look at two more verses, which happen to combine the two images:

The Lord will go forth like a mighty man, He will rouse up His zealous indignation and vengeance like a warrior; He will cry, yes, He will shout aloud, He will do mightily against His enemies. [Thus says the Lord] I have for a long time held My peace, I have been still and restrained Myself. Now I will cry out like a woman in travail, I will gasp and pant together (Isaiah 42:13-14 AMP).

Jesus is our example in fervent prayer. As I mentioned in the previous chapter, often He was *not* hushed and quiet when He prayed. He was stirred to the depths of His being, to the point that He could not suppress His explosive sighs. (Remember the story of Lazarus' death and resurrection in John 11:33-44.) The writer of Hebrews tells us that when Jesus walked the earth as the Son of Man, one way He showed His humanity was by the way He prayed: "In the days of His flesh [Jesus] offered up definite, special petitions...and supplications with strong crying and tears" (Hebrews 5:7a AMP).

"Strong crying and tears," especially the Greek term for it, gives the idea that He cried out loudly in prayer, even shouting and screaming.[6] It was the sound of the battlefield, a struggle of life and death. In no way was it timid or restrained.

The prayer of groaning brings deliverance from within and pushes back the pressures of darkness from without. Walls of resistance toward God are within each of us. We hardly see them, and we definitely cannot deliver ourselves from them, but this kind of prayer is higher than our understanding. It is larger than our limited comprehension, because it bypasses our minds and allows the Holy Spirit to move us into the freedom that God desires.

The prayer of groaning originates deep within our spirits. It is deep calling unto deep. It brings release from the grave clothes of dead works, stripping us so that we might be re-clothed by the Spirit of God. We long for even a foretaste of things to come, and we want to be prepared: "For indeed in this house we groan, longing to be clothed with our dwelling from heaven" (2 Cor. 5:2).

Travailing prayer comes before the promise is born, but not before the promise is conceived. Intimacy with God allows the "conception," as the promise is revealed and received into our spirits. But travail is how the birth is achieved. It opens up the way, removes the hindrances and constraints, and creates a broad "highway" for God's promise to be shown forth into the light of day (see Isa. 40:3).

When Elijah prayed, he gave it all he had (see James. 5:17). We have a description of his posture—he prayed with his face between his knees, crouched to the earth (see 1 Kings 18:42). That is a travailing posture. It's not the only kind of prayer; it's just one kind. But it's good to be aware of it in case the Holy Spirit brings you into the experience or you are in a place (hopefully a behind-the-scenes place) with other intercessors where it happens.

A good example of this kind of praying happened to me— along with a team of men—in 1986 in Haiti. I had gone there many times, but this time I was there with my friend, Mahesh Chavda, doing intercession before, during, and after his times of preaching. Many miracles had occurred, and many people had come to Jesus. Well, one time, in the middle of the night, I went with a small team up to an outlook over Port-au-Prince, the capital city. We felt that the Holy Spirit wanted us to go there. This was back when Jean-Claude "Baby Doc" Duvalier was dictator of the country, and he was as ruthless and decadent as his father ("Papa Doc") had been. The country had suffered for so long; it had become the poorest nation in the western hemisphere.

We got up in the middle of the night and went up to the overlook, burdened for the nation of Haiti. As a team, we had been praying and fasting. There in the darkness, overlooking the lights of the city, travailing prayer came upon us like a blanket, in a split second, as if the team members were one man. Instantly, we were praying in agreement in a prayer dimension that went beyond our understanding and previous experience. Our prayers went beyond the articulation of natural speech. We were like women in travail.

Being men, none of us had ever had children, so you could argue that I don't know what I'm talking about. But I had been with my wife four times in the birthing room, so I think I do know, at least partially, what it's like. One thing I know about it is that, once you're underway, you can't back up. You can't just put travail on "pause," even if you want to, anymore than you can stop labor and delivery from happening. You're committed to it, and you go with it, even if you don't look very calm, cool, and collected while it's happening.

We travailed until the Spirit lifted, and then we went back to where we had been staying. The next day, we heard the news: Baby Doc had fled the country. He was gone, headed for exile in France. His dictatorship had ended. This opened a season of mercy for the Haitians. It didn't solve every problem, but they did have the first democratic election in their history, and the rule of the Duvalier family had ended.

BE TENACIOUS

I want to mention one more thing. Travail takes time. You have to be tenacious. You will go through stretches when you are not crying out. In fact, nothing seems to be happening. It's more like being a watchman on a wall when nothing is happening. But you stay there. You don't abandon your post. You keep alert. You don't flag in your attention. You persevere. You need to be ready if the Holy Spirit is ready.

The psalmist wrote, "I pursued my enemies and overtook them, and I did not turn back until they were consumed" (Ps. 18:37). When did he quit? When the battle was over. He didn't quit in the middle, and he didn't take a break.

That's what Spirit-empowered prayer is like. The Holy Spirit's energy does not flag. When you're praying in the power of the Spirit, you will not give up. You will be able to go far beyond your normal ability to pray, even if you possess a lot of natural energy and zeal. You are breathing together, "con-spiring." As you do it, you get better at it. You keep pursuing your enemy until you over take him, and you keep laboring until you have a breakthrough.

When you undertake Spirit-empowered prayer, you operate with a watchman's anointing. You watch to see things in the Spirit. What is the enemy up to? What does God want to do about it? You take the keys of the Kingdom in your hand, and you bind up the darkness. You welcome the Spirit of the Lord's presence. You are vigilant and determined. You communicate with your fellow watchers. Together, you maintain the watch.

Father, I want to make a difference! I want to be one of the members of your spiritual armed forces, and I want to help to bring in Your Kingdom by force (see Matt. 11:12). Anoint me with Spirit-empowered prayer power that goes beyond my natural mind. Take me further in prayer than I have ever been before, for Your Kingdom's sake. I want to storm against the foe in prayer. Your Kingdom come, Your will be done, on earth as it is in Heaven. In Jesus' name, amen.

The Gathering Clouds, With Aspect Dark

The gathering clouds, with aspect dark,
A rising storm presage;
O! to be hid within the ark,
And sheltered from its rage!

See the commissioned angel frown!
That vial in his hand,
Filled with fierce wrath, is pouring down
Upon our guilty land!

Ye saints, unite in wrestling prayer;
If yet there may be hope;
Who knows but Mercy yet may spare,
And bid the angel stop!

So thunder, o'er the distant hills,
Gives but a murm'ring sound,
But as the tempest spreads, it fills,
And makes the welkin sound.

May we, at least, with one consent,
Fall low before the throne
With tears the nation's sins lament,
The churches, and our own.

The humble souls who mourn and pray,
The Lord approves and knows;
His mark secures them in the day
When vengeance strikes his foes.[1]

Chapter 4

INTERCESSORY PRAYER STORM IN TIMES OF CRISIS

With all prayer and petition pray at all times in the Spirit, and with this in view, be on the alert with all perseverance and petition for all the saints (Ephesians 6:18).

When I think about crisis intercession, I always remember Rees Howells, the famous Welsh intercessor who founded the Bible College of Wales at Swansea. His particular anointing provided the faith and the power to pray effectively for everything from world crises (notably during World War II) to financial crises at his school. The story of his life has been told widely.

When Rees Howells died in 1950, he passed on the leadership of the Bible College to his son Samuel, and his anointing came to Samuel as well. Over the decades, father and son led a small group of people, including many of the students and staff of the college, in crisis intercession. They prayed long and hard for breakthroughs, and they got verifiable results.

Samuel Howells died in 2004. But when he was 86, I was able to visit him at the Bible College. The Lord had given me a dream about "re-digging the wells of crisis intercession," but He had not told me how to do it. All I knew for sure was that I needed to visit the Bible College of Wales.

I was on a nationwide revival tour of Wales when I obtained a personal appointment with Mr. Howells (who rarely gave interviews to people). A friend from Indiana, Sue Kellough, who is a prophetess, went with me. I had one goal in mind for the appointment, and I was fastened on it—my goal was to receive an impartation of the Howells' anointing for crisis intercession.

Samuel Howells was a very distinguished gentleman. Though he was very frail, he carried a certain presence that I can only describe as the "fear of the Lord." We drank tea together and had a little tour of the building, including the "blue room" where so much of the praying had gone on. I could still feel a sort of residue of prayer in there.

I had one burning question, and I kept asking it: "How is it that your father got this level of revelation and authority for crisis intercession?" Our conversation kept going along, and I kept inserting this question whenever I could fit it in, but Mr. Howells kept ignoring it. Suddenly, the name of Leonard Ravenhill dropped into my mind. I knew Ravenhill was from England and that he was more or less a contemporary of Samuel's father Rees Howells. I said, "Oh, did you ever know the English evangelist named Leonard Ravenhill?" With that, he lit up, and his eyes sparkled.

"Oh, yes! He was one of our most frequent visitors here at the Bible School." He spoke of how they had loved him. I asked my question again. But again, instead of answering it, he asked me if I wanted another piece of cake. I wasn't getting anywhere.

Then my tenacious friend Sue got down on her knees and crawled over to right in front of the chair where the feeble old gentleman sat. She said, "Mr. Howells, you must understand. Our nation is in crisis. The world is in crisis. And we need the kind of authority in prayer that your father and those who prayed with him had...."

Then I turned to him for I think the fourth time, and I said, "How is it that your father got this level of revelation and authority for crisis intercession? Did it come by an angel who would give him these visions and words? Was it through dreams? How was it?"

This time, with a tear coming down his cheek, Samuel Howells said words to me that have marked me for life. He said, "You must understand. The Lord's servant was possessed by God."

That answered every question I had. We all started to weep together. Then, without asking, Mr. Howells laid his hands up on my shoulders, and he prayed that the Lord would give me and my friend Sue the type of authority and the type of history-making anointing in prayer that had rested on his father Rees Howells. I was humbled, and I received much more than I ever anticipated.

CALLING FORTH INTERCESSION IN PERILOUS TIMES

I wanted to start with that account, because I think that anyone who desires to undertake crisis intercession as part of the Prayer Storm, praying for crises as well as for revival, a youth awakening, and Israel, should be consumed with the cry: "Lord, *possess* me!"

You and I need to be possessed by the Spirit of God. We need Him to stir up the spiritual gifts within us. We need to go beyond our giftedness. We need His personal empowering. We need to be aroused by His grace to have a passion for Jesus, a passion for prayer, and a compassion for people greater than anything we've seen before. We need greater authority. We need the holy hand of the Almighty to come upon us, to over-shadow us.

So the question becomes, "How desperate *are* you?" How desperate *are* you for the Lord Himself, and how desperate are you on behalf of your family, your church, your region? How much do you desire a move of God, for the sakes of the people for whom you are a heavenly ambassador?

Desperate people pray desperate prayers, *extreme* prayers. And extreme results follow from extreme prayers. There has never been a period in history without extreme prayers preceding the fulfillment of the purposes of God. I don't know about you, but I want to be one of the "desperate people" of this generation, praying extreme prayers and getting extreme results.

SHAKING AND GLORY COME TOGETHER

The reason crisis intercession is so important is because it will always be in times of crisis—those times when everything gets shaken and people become more desperate—that God's glory will come. This means that disasters are actually good news, once you understand the principle. The prophet Haggai thundered:

> *This is what the Lord Almighty says: "In a little while I will once more shake the heavens and the earth, the sea and the dry land. I will shake all nations, and the desired of all nations will come, and I will fill this house with glory," says the Lord Almighty. "The silver is mine and the gold is mine," declares the Lord Almighty. "The glory of this present house will be greater than the glory of the former house," says the Lord Almighty* (Haggai 2:6-9a NIV).

This prophecy was fulfilled historically, but it has a present-day application as well, because we live in a time when we can expect ever-increasing glory to be released upon us and in us and through us—enough glory to make the former glory (which made it impossible for the priests to stand upright, you will remember) look like a mere *shadow* of the present glory.

The Lord Almighty will shake the heavens and the earth, the oceans and the land. He will shake the governments of nations. And this is good because it will make people desperate, and desperate people want more of God. When desperate people seek for more of God, His glory will "fill the Temple," which is no longer an edifice made of stone but which is now the Body of Christ throughout the earth.

In other words, crisis events around the globe, whether they are from natural disasters or human blunders, represent God's zeal to release His judgment on everything that hinders His love. And in His sovereignty and wisdom, God's judgments are always redemptive.

That's a massive statement right there. Most of us don't comprehend the truth of it. *God's judgments are always redemptive.* They're not the punishments of a mean and angry God who wants to wipe out sinners. Far from it. Every crisis is redemptive in nature, because through it, God can remove the hindrances that keep people from receiving His love. He wants to bring forth his spotless Bride. That is His passion.

The Church is quick to blame satan or sin for everything that seems bad. But we waffle with uncertainty when it comes to talking about God's role in disasters. I firmly believe that God is good all the time! How could He be good and at the same time allow evil to run rampant? He has the big picture. He is sovereign. He knows what it will take to wrap this thing up. Sometimes He works directly, and sometimes He works indirectly, as He allows other forces to work. But in every case, He rules. God rules. He sits on His throne, and He doesn't miss a thing.

Yet, He rules through His people! He rules, but He doesn't just keep the world moving like a bunch of puppets on strings. He is sovereign, but He does not rule all alone. He has established a role for people like us to extend the rule of His Kingdom, and it's called "prayer." He permits satan to express his rage—yet He has him on a leash! In the culmination of the end-times, those boundaries of satanic rage, which often seem too generous to us, will be further enlarged. (See Revelation 12:12.)

He permits man's sin to bring death and destruction. The free will He has given us allows us to make real choices that affect real life, choices that are sometimes good but often evil. Free-will choices provide a legal entry point for both angels and demons to be active in the natural realm. When people live in rebellion toward God, they open up legal entry points for demonic activity. Free-will decisions are important—they affect the quality of life in time and in eternity.

Rebellion produces an access point for evil as well. Obedience to God can open up portals to Heaven, as I shared in the last chapter of my book, *The Seer*. Jesus' model prayer, the one we call The Lord's Prayer, includes the words, "Your Kingdom come, Your will be done *on earth as it is in heaven*" (Matt. 6:10). As we align with His will, we allow Heaven to penetrate the earthly realm. When His will is being done, His Kingdom is being released in the here and now!

He also permits His creation to groan, and those "groanings" at times take on the form of violent weather patterns, earthquakes, and the like. There really is a connection between the conditions on the earth and the actions of the human race. The Bible establishes the fact that, when Adam sinned, a curse came upon the land (see Gen. 3). The curse has escalated as man's sin has escalated. Isaiah said that the earth's convulsions will increase as sin continues to ripen in the earth:

> *The earth is also defiled under its inhabitants, because they have transgressed the laws, changed the ordinance, broken the everlasting covenant. Therefore the curse has devoured the earth, and those who dwell in it are desolate. Therefore the inhabitants of the earth are burned, and few men are left.... The earth shall reel to and fro like a drunkard, and shall totter like a hut; its transgression shall be heavy upon it, and it will fall, and not rise again* (Isaiah 24:5-6,20 NKJV).

As a result of satan's temptation and human sin, the whole of creation suffers. The animal kingdom, plant kingdom, the atmosphere, even the rock under our feet, is under assault, is disintegrating. Paul wrote, "We know that the whole creation has been groaning as in the pains of childbirth right up to the present time" (Rom. 8:22 NIV).

The earth is waiting for something. You and I know what it is. It's Jesus, coming back to claim everything for Himself. But creation is also waiting for believing believers to take their places and to exercise authority in their delegated spheres of influence! It's all brought together as we keep reading the eighth chapter of Romans:

> *Not only* [creation]*, but we ourselves, who have the first-fruits of the Spirit, groan inwardly as we wait eagerly for our adoption as sons, the redemption of our bodies. For in this hope we were saved....In the same way, the Spirit helps us in our weakness. We do not know what we ought to pray for, but the Spirit Himself intercedes for us with groans that words cannot express. And He who searches*

our hearts knows the mind of the Spirit, because the Spirit intercedes for the saints in accordance with God's will (Romans 8:23-24,26-27 NIV).

That brings us back to intercession again. Do you see how important it is to take hold of your prayer assignments and to pray in the Spirit? You're helping open portals to Heaven so that the King can find faith on the earth. You are standing in the gap that separates Him from the world He wants to save. You're serving as a transmitter so that the language of Heaven can be heard on earth. Crisis times provide strategic opportunities.

STORM WARNINGS ARE BEING RELEASED

Another way of looking at this is to say that the shakings and rumblings and the storms themselves are really more like storm warnings. We can expect them to become more severe as the endtime draws closer. They are God's warnings; He's giving mankind an opportunity to respond to His offer of salvation. As He drops His plumb line (His Word and His character) into the midst of the nations, starting with the Church, everything that doesn't line up with it is going to contort and twist—that's why storms and crises occur. This is true in both the natural world and the spiritual world.

I can think of at least three kinds of storms. We need to respond to each one a little differently:

Storms of God's Judgment

When we are in the midst of storms of confusion and conflict, our response needs to be a cry for mercy. Broken and humbled, we confess our own sins, and we confess generational sins. We move into ambassadorial intercession, sometimes gathering with others in solemn assemblies. We need to be tenacious in our prayers.

Storms of Dark, Demonic Attack

When God allows storms of demonic attack, we need to eliminate any common ground with the enemy first and then stand in an authoritative place of intercession. We rebuke this kind of storm. These storms require steadfast faith, endurance, and boldness on the part of the intercessor. To use a King James word, we need to wax strong. We need to maintain our purity, relying on Jesus to clothe us in righteousness.

Storms of the Consequences of Sins

In order to press through storms that are the direct result of human sin, our own or that of a corporate body of people, we need to enter into identificational repentance, asking the Lord to forgive sins that we ourselves may not have committed. This requires humility, and it requires a lack of defensiveness. To do this, we follow the model of Daniel (and Ezra, Nehemiah, Esther, Moses, and others in the Old Testament). We also pray after the model of Jesus, "Forgive us our sins..." and "Your Kingdom come" (see Matt. 6:10,12).

No matter what kind of storm is battering us, we're after the same result: more of God's Kingdom. Each kind of storm requires a slightly different response, but in one way, they are all the same—they all lead to desperation. We're desperate for relief, and we're desperate for the Kingdom. We are not satisfied or comfortable. In our quest, we will do whatever it takes. We will pray 24/7, and we will fast and humble ourselves. Through it all, God forges character in us, which makes it possible for us to stand in prayer and to *keep* standing long and strong:

> *Therefore, take up the full armor of God, so that you will be able to resist in the evil day, and having done everything, to stand firm. Stand firm therefore, having girded your loins with truth, and having put on the breastplate of righteousness, and having shod your feet with the preparation of the gospel of peace; in addition to all, taking up the shield of faith with which you will be able to extinguish all the flaming arrows of the evil one. And take the helmet of salvation, and the sword of the Spirit, which is the word of God. With all prayer and petition pray at all times in the Spirit, and with this in view, be on the alert with all perseverance and petition for all the saints, and pray on my behalf, that utterance may be given to me in the opening of my mouth, to make known with boldness the mystery of the gospel, for which I am an ambassador in chains* (Ephesians 6:13-20).

THE ROLE OF GOD'S PEOPLE IN TIMES OF CRISIS

The majesty and mystery of intercession comes from the fact that God governs the universe in partnership with His people, through intercession. He partners with us just as He partners with His Son, Jesus, who intercedes perpetually:

> *He is also able to save to the uttermost those who come to God through Him, since He always lives to make intercession for them* (Hebrews 7:25 NKJV).

> *Ask of Me, and I will give You the nations for Your inheritance, and the ends of the earth for Your possession* (Psalm 2:8 NKJV).

God governs (releases His power to) the universe, which includes the nations of the earth, in cooperation with the prayers of believers like you and me. This is a mystery, but it is no less a fact.

God has already determined the primary events in His eternal plan. The Second Coming, the casting of satan into the lake of fire, the establishment of the new Heaven and new earth, and more will be accomplished regardless of what people or demons do. These events are non-negotiable.

However, He has chosen to give His people a dynamic role in determining some degree of the "quality of life" that we will experience in time and eternity. God has given each one of us a sphere of influence—our families, our everyday associations, and often beyond. We make a difference based on the meekness of our response to His grace and based on our partnership with God, particularly in prayer. We are, as Paul put it, "co-laborers with Christ" (2 Cor. 6:1).

This makes your place of prayer, whether it is a prayer closet, a mountain, or the driver's seat of your car, one of the governmental centers of the universe. Your prayers transcend time and distance. Paul could change the church in Ephesus by his prayers, even though he was far away in a dark prison in Rome at the time. Our prayers can be equally influential.

In response to our prayers, God opens doors of blessing and closes doors of oppression. There are certain blessings that God is prepared to bestow on us, but only if His people rise up in the intimate partnership of prayer to ask for them. It's easy to find examples of this throughout the Bible:

... You do not have because you do not ask (James 4:2).

But this kind does not go out except by prayer and fasting (Matthew 17:21).

Therefore the Lord longs to be gracious to you, and therefore He waits on high to have compassion on you....He will surely be gracious to you at the sound of your cry; when He hears it, He will answer you (Isaiah 30:18-19).

I sought for a man among them who would make a wall, and stand in the gap before Me on behalf of the land, that I should not destroy it; but I found no one (Ezekiel 22:30 NKJV).

Here you see it all: desperation, standing in the gap, taking authority. It's our job description as a participant in God's Prayer Storm!

And it's really true that the quality of our lives and the lives of the people around us depends on our response to God's promptings in the midst of these difficult circumstances. This life is not a practice game, although we do learn new things as long as we live. God has honored us with the dignity of the exercise of free will. We make real choices that make a real difference for good or for evil. If we choose righteously, then we have the power to open doors of blessing for others, as well as for ourselves. However, if we choose evil, we have the power to relegate people to the darkness.

I want to underline the importance of doing our part—using our free wills to obey and to pray. Some people "trust" the sovereignty of God, but it's often a non-biblical kind of trust, because they wrongfully trust God to accomplish the things that He has assigned to us. There are many things that God will not give us until we step out in obedient faith. Salvation itself is a good example. The Bible tells us that God wants all to be saved (see 1 Tim. 2:4), but practically speaking, this does not happen. Even though God wants everyone to be saved, some people reject the offer of salvation. God will not violate their free will, even when their salvation depends upon it. He is patient, and He will give us many opportunities to respond to Him (see 2 Pet. 3:8-9), but He will not complete the transaction if someone does not respond; He will not force the decision.

Now, at the same time, we cannot earn God's blessings by our prayers. That reflects a "works" mindset, permeated by a religious spirit. Rather, our prayers enable us to more fully cooperate with Him in releasing blessings. You see it particularly in corporate intercessory worship, which is the highest expression of the power of prayer to affect God's government in time and eternity. Corporate intercessory worship is far stronger than the combined strength of all the nuclear weapons that exist. And we are privileged—oh, so privileged!—to align ourselves with His purposes. He uses us as gatekeepers of His presence. Isn't that exciting?

CORPORATE INTERCESSORY WORSHIP

It's important to focus on corporate prayer—praying as a united group as a part of crisis intercession. Too many people, people who love God with all their hearts and who worship Him with passion, do not yet have a revelation of the authority and power that can be released by their corporate intercessory worship. They often understand the bridal paradigm, the language of intimacy and love for the Savior and Bridegroom, without understanding the purposes of the One to whom they are singing worship songs. His purpose is to win a people for Himself. His purpose is to be a Deliverer, a Redeemer. He is a Warrior as well as a Lover.

A lot of the time, a crisis, especially a crisis of national proportions, is too big for isolated intercessors to handle alone. At

this hour of history, what we need most is corporate intercessory worship and gathered-together ambassadorial intercession. What does this entail? It requires humility to pray in a
corporate way. Differences of style, doctrine, personality, and
culture make this paramount. Nobody is the star. People come
together in order to blend their voices as one. Together as a
Body of believers, the *group* stands in the gap. The individual
intercessors pool their insights and inspirations to declare back
to God biblical prayers and promises, to repent on behalf of
others, and to do whatever the situation requires of them.

Prophetic music and singing increase and hasten the
development of unity in the group, providing a sustainable way
in which thousands of people can feel the same thing for long
periods of time and creating an atmosphere out of which powerful forms of intercession can come.

I believe that God's primary call to a nation in crisis is for
people to gather together in solemn assemblies:

> *Therefore also now, saith the Lord, turn ye even to Me with
> all your heart, and with fasting, and with weeping, and
> with mourning: And rend your heart, and not your gar-
> ments, and turn unto the Lord your God: for He is gra-
> cious and merciful, slow to anger, and of great kindness,
> and repenteth Him of the evil. Who knoweth if He will
> return and repent, and leave a blessing behind Him; even a
> meat offering and a drink offering unto the Lord your God?
> Blow the trumpet in Zion, sanctify a fast, call a solemn
> assembly: Gather the people... (Joel 2:12-16 KJV).*

Corporate intercessory worship stops the enemy from a
rampage of destruction, and it releases God's judgment:

> *Let the high praises of God be in their mouth, and a two-
> edged sword in their hand, to execute vengeance on the*

nations, and punishments on the peoples; to bind their kings with chains, and their nobles with fetters of iron; to execute on them the written judgment—this honor have all His saints (Psalm 149:6-9 NKJV).

Corporate intercession is powerful!

OLD TESTAMENT EXAMPLES OF CRISIS INTERCESSION

As we go through times of crisis and transition, the enemy tries to take advantage of the situation by bringing confusion and discouragement. We need gifts of discernment and wisdom in order to discern the difference between the enemy's wrath and God's righteous judgment. We need to pray prior to receiving revelation, and then we need to act or pray according to the revelation that God sends. (See Revelation 8:4-5.)

God is the same yesterday, today, and forever (see Heb. 13:8). Therefore, not only does He want to hear the voices of intercessors in the present day or since the time of Jesus, but He has always wanted to hear and answer prayer. The anointing that we receive today for crisis intercession is the same anointing that we see in operation throughout the Old Testament. Let's look at a few examples.

Abraham's Bartering

Very early in the ancient texts, we find the story of Abraham standing in the gap for the people of Sodom and Gomorrah. God wanted to destroy these twin cities, because they were filled with wickedness. But Abraham, it seems in part because of his nephew Lot, had the courage to bargain with God, just as one might bargain in the marketplace. "Will you save the cities if 50 righteous men are found there?... if 40 are found...30? ...." And on down to ten righteous men. As it turned out, God could not find even ten righteous men in the city, and Abraham's nephew and his daughters barely escaped before God's fiery judgment rained down and utterly destroyed it (see Gen. 18:16-33; 19:27-29).

Abraham's conversation with God shows us that we too can exercise this option at times. God does not spurn "bartering" prayers. Perhaps there is a principle here: When man quits, God quits. Therefore, keep on asking!

Rachel's Desperate Cry

What moves the heart of God? Faith does. So does humility. So does desperation. Rachel was desperate—for a child. She was barren. "Now when Rachel saw that she bore Jacob no children, Rachel envied her sister, and said to Jacob, "Give me children, or else I die!" (Gen. 30:1 NKJV). Hers was a personal desperation, but it moved the heart of God no less than as if it had been the desperation of an entire people group—which in a way it was, considering the vast number of Rachel's descendents.

That phrase, "give me children, or else I die," has been illumined throughout revival seasons as people have picked it up as a great prayer for children to be reborn into the Kingdom of God. John Knox, the great reformer in Scotland, was given this phrase to cry out for his nation, and he was heard praying it out loud as he walked in the hills.

Moses' Intercessory Acts

Most of us are very familiar with Moses' story, so I will just highlight a few of the many times that he and other leaders performed intercessory acts in obedience to God: the parting of the Red Sea (see Exod. 14), the bitter waters made sweet (see

Exod. 15:25), Aaron and Hur standing with Moses as intercessory helpers during the battle with the Amalekites (see Exod. 17:8-16), and Moses sending Aaron running through the people with his censor to stop the plague (see Num. 16:41-50). These words paint pictures of Moses as intercessor:

> *Moses sought the favor of the Lord his God. "O Lord," he said, "why should Your anger burn against Your people, whom You brought out of Egypt with great power and a mighty hand? Why should the Egyptians say, 'It was with evil intent that He brought them out, to kill them in the mountains and to wipe them off the face of the earth'? Turn from Your fierce anger; relent and do not bring disaster on Your people. Remember Your servants Abraham, Isaac and Israel, to whom You swore by Your own self: 'I will make your descendants as numerous as the stars in the sky and I will give your descendants all this land I promised them, and it will be their inheritance forever.'" Then the Lord relented and did not bring on His people the disaster He had threatened* (Exodus 32:11-14 NIV).

> *Once again I fell prostrate before the Lord for forty days and forty nights; I ate no bread and drank no water, because of all the sin you had committed, doing what was evil in the Lord's sight and so provoking Him to anger. I feared the anger and wrath of the Lord, for He was angry enough with you to destroy you. But again the Lord listened to me* (Deuteronomy 9:18-19 NIV).

Moses was an intercessor *par excellence.* Let us learn from his model!

Gideon's 300 Men

Do you remember the process of elimination that God led Gideon through? The story is in the seventh chapter of the Book of Judges. In the end, the only men who were allowed to become part of Gideon's army were the ones who, when they came to the water to drink, knelt on one knee and brought the water up to their mouths to drink it. In other words, they were watchful, keeping one eye on what was going on around them, even as they drank. They were "worshipful watchers," down on one knee but with eyes open, alert to danger.

I feel a real connection with Gideon. In fact, I feel that there has been a kind of a "Gideon anointing" on my life, as I (fully aware of my insignificance and smallness) raise up an army of "watchers" who will march on their knees, alert to threats and strong in the Lord. In fact, I want to see one million worshipful watchers arise across the globe and join us in Prayer Storm, in the "hour that changes the world." Will you be one of them?

Hannah's Cry for a Son

Hannah was in a personal crisis. Her chief rival, her husband's other wife, Peninnah, was able to have children, but Hannah was barren. She was desperate for a child. So one year, when the family group traveled to worship and offer sacrifices at Shiloh, Hannah, in great travail of soul, bargained with God in prayer, promising to dedicate her child to the Lord's service if He would open her womb (see 1 Sam. 1). As she had prayed, it happened, and her son Samuel became a priest, judge, and prophet who was also an intercessor and was so very important to the history of Israel. Hannah's prayer was motivated by personal desperation but, as often happens, God's answer to her prayer fulfilled a much bigger destiny. It will be the same in your life as well!

David's Victory Over Goliath

David's prophetic act of intercession was to choose to walk in his own anointing rather than in the armor borrowed from Saul. In First Samuel, we read what he did:

> *David fastened on his sword over the tunic and tried walk-*
> *ing around, because he was not used to them. "I cannot go*
> *in these," he said to Saul, "because I am not used to them."*
> *So he took them off. Then he took his staff in his hand,*
> *chose five smooth stones from the stream, put them in the*
> *pouch of his shepherd's bag and, with his sling in his hand,*
> *approached the Philistine* (1 Samuel 17:39-40 NIV).

In essence, David could not wear the armor of a previous generation. To respond to the taunts of the enemy, David had to take what he had already experienced (being a shepherd, a lion-killer, a psalmist, and a releaser of declarations) and walk in it. He took more than one stone in his arsenal, but his weapon was one he was already familiar with. Are you using your tried and tested weapons in battle, or are you relying only upon the history of others?

Elijah's Travail

At Elijah's word, the rain had stopped completely (see 1 Kings 17:1). After three years of desperate drought, God told him to "pray it back" (see 1 Kings 18). First, he and God won the impressive victory over the prophets of Baal, and then, still up on Mount Carmel, he began to pray for rain. He had to be persistent. Even his posture, with his head down between his knees, bespoke the travail of childbirth. After he had his servant check the empty sky several times, a small cloud began to form. Eventually his prayers were answered when the sky released heavy rains. Elijah had to be sure of what he was hearing from God. Many lives depended on it. And yes, many lives will depend upon our prayers as well!

Elisha's Prophetic Actions

Elisha had asked for a double portion of Elijah's spirit, and he got it. As we know from reading the account of his life in the Book of Second Kings, he demonstrated an unparalleled combination of prophetic intercessory actions. (For example, read about the time he lay on top of the Shunnamite boy to bring him back to life in Second Kings 4:32-35.) Oh, that the leaders of the Church would arise with that same resurrection power, breathe on the sickened, dead Body, and breathe new life back into the Church!

Another time, he prayed and got the revelation from God to throw flour into the pot of poisonous stew so that nobody would be harmed (see 2 Kings 4:38-41). Oh, that the Spirit of faith and revelation would arise whenever a crisis occurs so that what is intended for harm will instead be turned to the good!

In a time of severe crisis, when military defeat seemed imminent, Elisha prayed that his servant's eyes would be opened to see the array of heavenly forces that were amassed on the hills (see 2 Kings 6:17). After Elisha delivered what amounted to a prophetic declaration, the enemy was defeated by the power of God (without any physical warfare).

Elisha's whole life was filled with this sort of crisis intervention. As a prophet, his actions and advice often opened the way to the future fulfillment of God's will. I'm thinking of the time, very near the end of his life, when he told King Joash to shoot arrows out of the open window to predict his victory over Syria (see 2 Kings 13:15-19). After one arrow was shot, he told him to strike the ground with the rest. But instead of striking the ground time after time, the king struck it only three times and then stopped. If only he had persevered and kept striking! That's the lesson that we as intercessors can learn from the story: persist, endure, continue to pursue the enemy, and never give up!

Nehemiah's Burden for Restoration

Nehemiah was the king's cupbearer, which means that he was in the king's service and that he had his ear. In much the same way, we as intercessors have the King's ear, and we can exercise the right combination of boldness and innovation. Nehemiah both prayed for favor and then asked for it outright, asking for the privilege of rebuilding the walls of Jerusalem and repenting on behalf of the people for their sins (see Neh. 1:6-7). Favor was granted, and great progress was made. May we as intercessors be consumed with such a burden for the Kingdom of God that we too will be able to rebuild the walls of protection around our people. Let us be modern-day cupbearers and stand before the King of Kings!

Esther's Divine Appointment

In a time of crisis, when genocide was being proposed against the Jewish people, Esther found herself in a position "for such a time as this," in which she could intervene—with strategies and circumstances that only God could have supplied— to reverse the death order (see the whole Book of Esther). May the Esther anointing be released again in our day. In this generation, may the worldwide Bride of Christ be positioned and prepared to rise up in her full beauty to stand in the face of evil.

May the corporate Esther, the Body of Christ, arise and take a stand with Israel in the Last Days!

Isaiah's Persistent Petitioning

True, authentic revival comes about when God's people allow their inner beings to be filled with that which is in God's heart and when the agony of His oppressed people grips their hearts so that they cry out as women in travail. Not only did Isaiah travail in prayer, I like to say that Isaiah "lived in the *until* clauses," praying in persistent faith during the gaps between the revelation and the fulfillment:

> *For Zion's sake I will not hold My peace, and for Jerusalem's sake I will not rest,* **until** *her righteousness goes forth as brightness, and her salvation as a lamp that burns. The Gentiles shall see your righteousness, and all kings your glory. You shall be called by a new name, which the mouth of the Lord will name* (Isaiah 62:1-2 NKJV).

> *On your walls, O Jerusalem, I have appointed watchmen; all day and all night they will never keep silent. You who remind the Lord, take no rest for yourselves; and give Him no rest* **until** *He establishes and makes Jerusalem a praise in the earth* (Isaiah 62:6-7).

Jeremiah's Warnings and Pleas

Of Josiah, Jeremiah prophesied, "'He pled the cause of the afflicted and needy; then it was well. Is not that what it means to know Me?' declares the Lord" (Jer. 22:16 NASB). This is laden with revelation. Crying out for the sake of the oppressed is what? —to know God! Knowing Him means having His heart for the needy, which in turns means that you plead their cause.

Josiah carried God's burning desire for justice, and God endorsed him for it through Jeremiah's words—at the same time warning Josiah's sons to stop their evil ways.

If we let God give us prayer assignments, something about it goes beyond an assignment. If you will let the burden hook you, you'll be reeled into something more than assignment; you'll be reeled into the very heart of God. You will know His mercy, feel His burdens, carry His burning desire for justice. Justice is the cry of this generation. Let judicial intercessors arise for Jesus Christ's sake!

Daniel's Model of Character and Authority

Not caring if his actions resulted in a death sentence, Daniel maintained his prayer life before God. Not only that, but he also pled for the fulfillment of former prophecies about God's people, with whom he was in exile in Babylon. He picked up the baton that had been given to the previous generation 70 years earlier, not resting in the assumption that God would simply act to fulfill His Word, now that the time had come. Instead of passively waiting, he confessed generational sins in order to remove the blockages to the completion of God's promises. His consistency, his faith, his humility, and his obedience to God remain as one of the finest examples of godly character in the Bible. And his prayers were answered as He reminded God of His Word.

Joel's Trumpet Sound

The prophet Joel didn't know that his call would echo through the centuries to the present day. His call to pray, fast, weep, and travail has been used in the past and will be used again to change times of desolation into times of restoration through holy consecration. I quoted his summons a little earlier in this chapter in the context of talking about solemn assemblies. Still today, Joel's prophetic voice trumpets over the tumult of evil and summons the people of God—priests, prophets, and warriors—to the front lines. Do you hear Joel's trumpet being sounded? Answer the call!

Amos—Holding Off Judgment

The prophet Amos interceded when he received visionary revelations, and his prayers are perhaps the premiere examples of prophetic crisis intercession in the Bible. Wherever the judgment of God had been pronounced, Amos set himself to interceding until the Lord relented, and His hand of judgment was lifted. Whether it was judgment by locusts, judgment by fire, or judgment by plumb line, Amos said to the Lord, "Sovereign Lord, forgive! How can Jacob survive? He is so small!" And every time, incredibly, "the Lord relented. 'This will not happen,' the Lord said" (see Amos 7:1-9 NIV). Like Amos, we need to be prophetic intercessors who will hold off wars, terrorist attacks, volcanic eruptions, earthquakes, tsunamis, and other natural calamities by calling on God to release His mercy. Like Amos, we need discernment to be able to cooperate with Him in matters such as these.

New Testament Examples of Crisis Intercession

I have barely scratched the surface of all the possible Old Testament examples of crisis intercession. I just gave you glimpses so that you can have a collection of templates to work from. Though it may look as if the Old Testament is my main source of examples (compared to what you are about to see in the rest of this chapter), that's mostly because the Old Testament is a lot longer than the New Testament and is filled with a lot more of the classic stories about God's intervention in times of crisis.

However, if you read between the lines of the New Testament, while bearing intercession in mind, the entire collection of books and letters turns out to be one long account of effective crisis intervention through prayer. That's because the whole New Testament is about Jesus, the greatest Intercessor and Intervener of them all! Not only did He come to earth as a man in order to redeem the human race, and not only does the resurrected Jesus continually intercede at the Father's side, but Jesus also showed us how to pray in specific situations. He was in constant communication with His Father. He was ready every time that He and the disciples confronted a crisis.

Jesus Calms the Storm

For example, look at the account of the calming of the storm (see Matt. 8:23-27). The storm was so violent that the boat was about to sink. Jesus spoke to the storm and rebuked it, and immediately the wind and the waves died down. The disciples were astonished, saying, "What kind of man is this? Even the winds and the waves obey Him" (Matt. 8:27 NIV). Why don't we exercise the same level of apostolic authority today? If we did, even fervent Muslims, Hindus, and atheists would say, "I believe!" No longer would people name the name of Jesus as a lucky charm or as their divine "fire escape," because He would be a living reality in their lives.

The Fervent Intercession of the Early Church

The members of the early church came under severe persecution individually and collectively. To be known as a follower of Jesus Christ was a life-and-death matter. Did the believers run away and hide? No, they stayed and prayed. But they didn't pray for protection as much as they prayed to be effective witnesses in the midst of the harassment. Here's how they prayed:

> *"Now, Lord, consider their threats and enable Your servants to speak Your word with great boldness. Stretch out Your hand to heal and perform miraculous signs and wonders through the name of Your holy servant Jesus." After they prayed, the place where they were meeting was shaken. And they were all filled with the Holy Spirit and spoke the word of God boldly* (Acts 4:29-31 NIV).

They prayed, and the building was shaken. This wasn't just another natural earth tremor. This was like a heavenly embrace. At the same moment that the house started shaking, they were so re-filled with the Holy Spirit that they began to preach. Never mind that the walls were showing cracks. Never mind the new threats that their enemies would utter the next morning when they went out into the streets. God was in the house, and miracles were in the air!

Peter's Release

Do you remember this line from the story of Peter's miraculous release from prison? "So Peter was kept in the prison, but prayer for him was being made fervently by the church to God" (Acts 12:5). They were doing the *only* thing that could make a difference. They got together, and they prayed. Already James, the brother of John, had been killed. To keep Peter from being next on the hit list, the Church prayed. It probably wasn't a huge group, no more of them than would fit into a house. But that didn't slow them down. They prayed fervently. No one was more surprised then they were (well, maybe Peter was more surprised) when an angel came and led him out of the extra-secure prison (see Acts 12:6-17). It was no problem for the angel. The Church had prayed, and he had been summoned in response. As a direct result of Peter's deliverance from his captors, he went on to preach the Gospel and strengthen the Church. Faced with crisis, the Church felt that Peter was irreplaceable. They went to God about it. God agreed and set him free so that he could continue to minister in Jesus' name. We can do the same!

Paul and Silas Rock the Dungeon

The early Christians certainly kept jailers busy. Remember the time when Paul and Silas were imprisoned together in Philippi? (See Acts 16:22-33.) I think this is a great example of the power of intercession through worship. Paul and Silas were singing hymns and worshiping God, even in the depths of the dungeon. An earthquake rocked the place, and their shackles fell off. Locked doors were thrown open. This was no coincidental earthquake. As a result of this miraculous intervention from God, the jailer and his entire household became Christians.

Paul Requests Prayers

We get used to these stories. We know they have good endings. But the people involved did not know. Like us today, they had only the negative evidence before them and their raw faith. Every single time, they prayed—and they often requested supporting prayer. Far from passively assuming that their circumstances were already decided by fate or a remote and sovereign godhead figure, they engaged God in passionate conversation about whatever was happening. Paul specifically requested prayer often. He knew full well that God had chosen to allow believers to be His co-laborers and that God wanted to hear prayers:

Pray in the Spirit on all occasions with all kinds of prayers and requests. With this in mind, be alert and always keep

*on praying for all the saints. Pray also for me, that when-
ever I open my mouth, words may be given me so that I will
fearlessly make known the mystery of the gospel, for which
I am an ambassador in chains. Pray that I may declare it
fearlessly, as I should* (Ephesians 6:18-20 NIV).

POSTSCRIPTS TO THE NEW TESTAMENT

In our own day, we can point to many true stories of the
power of crisis intercession. I started this chapter with the
account of my visit to Samuel Howells in Wales, and I mentioned his father's dedication to intercession. Rees Howells
always did more than merely pray whatever occurred to him. He
ardently sought to know God's heart before he prayed, and then
he would lead his fellow intercessors in praying strategically
and relentlessly until a breakthrough was achieved. They would
often receive revelation about the enemy's plans and God's
strategies—quite independently of news reports—and they
would pray accordingly.

One such example of this happened before World War II,
when Hitler was beginning to make moves against certain countries. In what became known as the Munich crisis, Hitler was
being advised to attack Great Britain, which was unprepared.
War seemed inevitable, and the leaders of Great Britain called
for a day of prayer. The intercessors of the Bible College of
Wales rose to the challenge, praying not only on the designated
day, but for many days.

It was a clear case of spiritual warfare between the forces
who were urging Hitler to strike and the Holy Spirit's forces,
which included a small army of intercessors. As the prayer-
battle reached a crescendo, the one prayer that Rees Howells
felt led to pray was, "Lord, bend Hitler." In the Spirit, he knew
when the point of victory came. In fact, he was so confident in

this that he organized—and advertised—a day of praise and thanksgiving "because God has again averted a European War." On that day, the people of the town joined the Bible College in celebration, even though the news about Hitler remained the same. However, just the day after the celebration, the Munich Pact was signed. It was true; war had been averted miraculously.[2]

We could share stories for a month and not cover all of the wonderful results of prayer in times of crisis. God is not just the God of Rees Howells or Isaiah or the apostle Peter. He is the God of each and every one of us, and He wants to anoint us and give us prayer assignments. He wants to send us places that nobody has ever prayed before. He is looking for a humble, contrite people who know the times in which they live and who know what the Lord requires of His people in such a time. He is looking for people who want to learn about confession, repentance, and intercession. He is urging us to cultivate an authentic spirit of faith mingled with the spirit of revelation, both of which come straight from the heart of the Father. Then He can send us straight into the face of the enemy. We can say, "This far, and no more! I'm taking this back for the Kingdom of the King!"

Here I am, Lord! Use me. Use us. Let crisis intervention arise through intercession for such a time as this. Teach me to stand in the gap so that Your Kingdom can come and Your will can be done on earth as it is in Heaven. Capture me for Your holy purposes, in Jesus' holy name. Amen.

They Fasted

On Sinai's mount, with radiant face,
To intercede for heaven's grace
Upon a stubborn, wayward race,
He fasted.

Once lifted from the miry clay,
When opposition came his way
This soldier-king would often pray
With fasting.

A seer, possessed of vision keen,
Who told the troubled king his dream,
Had light on God's prophetic scheme
Through fasting.

The prophetess in temple court
Beheld the Babe the two had brought;
For Him she long had prayed and sought,
With fasting.

He came to break the yoke of sin,
But ere His mission could begin
He met the foe and conquered him
With fasting.

"Set these apart," the Spirit bade.
A spring, that soon vast rivers made,
Broke open by men who as they prayed
Were fasting.

"So shall they fast when I am gone;
Was this no word to act upon?
Ask countless saints who fought and won
With fasting.

When we shall stand on that great day
And give account, what shall we say,
If He should ask us, "Did you pray—
With fasting?"

(Author unknown)

— 118 —

Chapter 5

PRAYER WITH FASTING—GOD'S WAY

"Yet even now," declares the Lord, "Return to Me with all your heart, and with fasting, weeping and mourning; and rend your heart and not your garments." Now return to the Lord your God, for He is gracious and compassionate, slow to anger, abounding in lovingkindness and relenting of evil. Who knows whether He will not turn and relent and leave a blessing behind Him...? (Joel 2:12-14).

As we see throughout the Bible, fasting was a common practice among the Jews as well as among the early Christians. It has remained a common spiritual discipline throughout Christian history. However, in the modern Western world, it has fallen out of favor for obvious reasons—our high standard of living has created a culture of plenty and instant gratification. Fasting represents the opposite. In this chapter, however, I want to restore fasting to the prayer-equation, lest we forget about it. We can't talk about having a Prayer Storm without talking about fasting as well.

Although we're familiar with the term *spiritual discipline*, I want to modify it somewhat. A few years ago, the Holy Spirit said to me, repeatedly, "You don't have enough discipline to have a spiritual discipline." I had to agree! I hardly knew anybody who seemed to have enough personal discipline to maintain any kind of a rigorous spiritual discipline. Then He said to me, "It's not a spiritual discipline, it's a spiritual *privilege*." That completely shifts the mindset, doesn't it? Yes, discipline is involved, of course. Consistency is important. But it's the grace that God supplies that makes it possible. I can only fast because God touches my heart and gives me revelation. Otherwise, I end up fasting as sort of a religious arm-twisting exercise, and that doesn't win anybody anything.

When I benefit from the grace that He gives, and I receive His heart, which He imparts, then I see the divine privilege of co-laboring with Him. If intercessory prayer is co-laboring with Him, how much more then is fasting? It's one of the greatest privileges in the Kingdom to be able to seek His favor in this way.

Moses sought the favor of God over the impending destruction of Israel. In Deuteronomy 9, we see that Moses fasted and prayed for 40 days. That's a long time to pray—especially since he had just completed a 40-day stretch on the mountain. Really, this was a back-to-back set of 40-day fasts—but we see that he added fasting to his prayer in order to reinforce his cry concerning God's wrath against Israel. It worked. God relented, and the people were saved.

Leaders use Moses' prayer and fasting as an example when they call solemn assemblies in which they stipulate that people must enter into a corporate time of not only praying but also fasting. (It's not always only a food fast; the people often abstain from some of their regular activities as well.) To me, fasting illustrates a spiritual principle that you can't find in one tidy little verse but that is illustrated throughout Scripture—man's sacrifice (which includes a right heart attitude) releases God's power.

THE BIBLICAL ORIGINS OF FASTING

I referred above to Moses' 40-day fast for the people of Israel. That is the second fast mentioned in the Bible; the first one was the one that Moses had just completed on Mount Sinai, during which God had given him the Ten Commandments on stone tablets and the directions for building the tabernacle (see Exod. 34:28; Deut. 9:9). Moses made it clear what he did while he was on the mountain meeting with God: "...I neither ate bread nor drank water" (Deut. 9:9).

In English, the words *fast* and *fasting* come from the Anglo-Saxon word *faest*, which means "firm" or "fixed." The connection to food is that the word *faesten* means to hold oneself from eating food.[1] In the Hebrew, the root word is *tsum*, which refers to self-denial.[2] Most likely, the practice of fasting began as a loss of appetite during times of great distress. We can pull out at least three examples of this kind of stress-induced fasting from the Old Testament:

- Hannah was greatly distressed due to her barrenness, so "she wept and did not eat" (1 Sam. 1:7 NKJV).

- King Ahab, when he failed to obtain Naboth's vineyard, lay down on his bed, turned his face to the wall, and "would eat no food" (1 Kings 21:4 NKJV).

- David used fasting to express his grief at Abner's death: "When all the people came to persuade David to eat food while it was still day, David took an oath, saying, 'God do so to me, and more also, if I taste bread or anything else till the sun goes down'" (2 Sam. 3:35 NKJV).

Fasting is a natural expression of human grief, and it became customary to fast to fend off God's anger. Eventually, fasting became a way of making one's petition more effective before God. Fasting was practiced on a large scale to prevent national disaster. It was implemented to request divine protection or to circumvent the judgment of God because of sin. Therefore, it became a normal practice for a group of people to combine confession of sin, sorrow, and intercession with fasting.

The only required group fast in the Old Testament was on the Day of Atonement, on which the High Priest would offer acts of sacrifice for the sins of the people. The people fasted for self-examination and to demonstrate their remorse:

> *Aaron shall bring the bull of the sin offering, which is for himself, and make atonement for himself and for his house, and shall kill the bull as the sin offering which is for himself.... Then he shall kill the goat of the sin offering, which is for the people, bring its blood inside the veil, do with that blood as he did with the blood of the bull, and sprinkle it on the mercy seat and before the mercy seat.... Aaron shall lay both his hands on the head of the live goat, confess over it all the iniquities of the children of Israel, and all their transgressions, concerning all their sins, putting them on the head of the goat, and shall send it away into the wilderness by the hand of a suitable man.... This shall be a statute forever for you: In the seventh month, on the tenth day of the month, you shall afflict your souls, and do no work at all, whether a native of your own country or a stranger who dwells among you. For on that day the priest shall make atonement for you, to cleanse you, that you may be clean from all your sins before the Lord. It is a sabbath of solemn rest for you, and you shall afflict your souls. It is a statute forever* (Leviticus 16:11,15,21,29-31 NKJV).

The people were required to fast at this time; it was not optional. Although, in our day, we think of fasting as an individual decision, I believe that people can still be told to fast as a matter of obedience in times of exceptional crisis.

As we refer to it today, fasting is a deliberate act, not an involuntary one that results from distress or famine. Fasting means voluntary abstinence from food (or other personal appetites) for spiritual purposes. Fasting helps a person focus his or her attention on God, because it quiets the soul so that a person can hear God's voice better. It represents a very real sacrifice that releases power or a display of God's blessing—not that fasting will "buy" us something from God, but it aligns us with His purposes and will, and that is powerful.

Fasting is a key to the supernatural. It releases God's presence. Because of Jesus' death and resurrection, we live under the New Covenant, and believers already have access to the throne. We no longer fast to obtain forgiveness or atonement. However, we can definitely fast for greater *consecration*. Just as the High Priest, on the Day of Atonement, would go behind the veil where the presence of God manifested Himself, so we also can fast to taste the manifested presence of God. The Old Testament accounts foreshadow a New Testament reality, and part of that reality involves the release of God's presence.

The evangelist Charles Finney consecrated himself with fasting. I believe he had discovered a key of understanding. He would say that if he could sense the power lifting off him when he preached, the spirit of conviction did not operate in as full a manner. He would then consecrate himself with fasting until the presence of God returned and brought with it a greater conviction and greater dimensions of power.[3] When we consider crisis intervention and all the other things that we need to pray about, we realize that the release of God's presence in our time-space world is the determining factor.

Fasting in the New Testament

Fasting was well-established within Jewish tradition by the time of Jesus. Unfortunately, it had become part of the "works" mindset of the established authorities, the Pharisees, as evidenced by these verses from Luke:

> *The Pharisee took his stand ostentatiously and began to pray thus before and with himself: God, I thank You that I am not like the rest of men—extortioners (robbers), swindlers [unrighteous in heart and life], adulterers—or even like this tax collector here. I fast twice a week; I give tithes of all that I gain* (Luke 18:11-12 AMP).

We know from that revealing passage of Scripture that the Pharisees fasted twice a week, and it is believed that they fasted on Tuesdays and Thursdays. An early bishop of the Church, Epiphanius of Salamis (born in A.D. 315) stated, "Who does not know that the fasts of the fourth and sixth days of the week [i.e., Wednesdays and Fridays] are observed by Christians throughout the world?"[4] These days were chosen to prevent confusion with the Pharisees' days, Tuesdays and Thursdays.

We know that John the Baptist fasted regularly, being a Nazarite from birth who came in the spirit of Elijah (see Num. 6:2-8; Matt. 9:14-15; Luke 1:15-17). A *Nazarite* was "a person of the vow," and fasting was an important component of their sacrificial lifestyle.

With Jesus, however, an important contrast was established. Although He began His public ministry with an extended observance of the annual Jewish fast on the Day of Atonement, He gave very few specific guidelines to His disciples concerning fasting. He did say that their fasting should be different from that of the Pharisees, namely that it should be practiced to be seen by God and not to impress other people:

> *Whenever you fast, do not put on a gloomy face as the hypocrites do, for they neglect their appearance so that they will be noticed by men when they are fasting. Truly I*

say to you, they have their reward in full. But you, when you fast, anoint your head and wash your face so that your fasting will not be noticed by men, but by your Father who is in secret; and your Father who sees what is done in secret will reward you (Matthew 6:16-18).

He also made a particular point of challenging John's Nazarite-influenced disciples with the new idea of what we now call the Bridegroom fast (see Matt. 9:15). I will save a full discussion of this kind of fasting for later in the chapter, but for now I want to make the point that Jesus was promoting fasting *as an act of worship.* He brought His Kingdom to earth, and the response of those He came to save is to humble themselves, often with fasting, and to consecrate their whole lives to His service.

After Jesus' death and resurrection and the establishment of the early Church, fasting was carried out both as a way to underline consecration and as a regular reminder of humble dependence upon God's saving grace. Notice the matter-of-fact inclusion of fasting as part of the life of the Church and its leaders:

While they were ministering to the Lord and fasting, the Holy Spirit said, "Set apart for Me Barnabas and Saul for the work to which I have called them" (Acts 13:2).

But we commend ourselves in every way as [true] servants of God: through great endurance, in tribulation and suffering, in hardships and privations, in sore straits and calamities, in beatings, imprisonments, riots, labors, sleepless watching, hunger (2 Corinthians 6:4-5 AMP).

As the Church grew and spread, fasting continued to be a regular feature of the time of preparation leading up to Easter, which evolved into the 40-day season of partial fasting known as Lent. In the second and third centuries, fasting was instituted as one of the elements of a new believer's preparation for water baptism. As I have already mentioned, fasting two days a week was a common practice among individual Christians. They took their faith seriously!

Moving forward throughout the centuries, we see that the discipline of fasting has almost always played an important role in helping to bring in reforms and revivals. All of the founders of the various monastic movements practiced fasting as a regular part of their lifestyles. Each of the 16th-century reformers (as well as the earlier ones) practiced fasting; so did the leaders of the evangelical "great awakenings." John Wesley would not ordain a man to the ministry unless he fasted two days every week. Jonathan Edwards is known to have fasted before he preached his now-famous sermon, "Sinners in the Hands of an Angry God." During the North American laymen's prayer revival in 1859, Christians skipped lunch in order to attend prayer meetings. In all of these cases, fasting was an important element for the advancement of God's Kingdom in particular locales.

THE WAYS AND MEANS OF FASTING

Just to make sure we're all talking about the same thing, I want to run through some details about fasting. Not all fasts are as complete as Esther's fast (see Esther 4:16; Acts 9:9), in which she and others refrained from all food and all liquid for three days, though I do think this sort of fast has a place in Prayer Storm. It's a desperate act for desperate times, and the Spirit can and does lead people do to it. I've done it myself more than once.

Most of the time, a *regular fast* involves refraining from all food and drink except water; no nourishment is consumed, including juice, alcohol, or sweeteners. That's the kind of fast that Jesus undertook during His temptation in the wilderness (see Matt. 4:2). Although this form of fasting may seem extreme to someone who has never done it, it's quite feasible. A regular fast can last anywhere from one day to several weeks.

A *partial fast* means what it sounds like it means—you refrain from part of your nourishment. You may decide to skip a certain meal every day, or you may restrict your intake of certain foods. Daniel and his friends refrained from eating meat and rich foods. Their partial fast consisted of a vegetable-only diet (see Dan. 1:8-16). You decide what to do as God leads. A partial fast is a great first step toward a more complete fast. Even if health reasons prohibit you from undertaking a regular fast, God will bless the partial fast that you choose.

In a *liquid fast,* you partake of liquids such as juices, clear broth, and water, but you take no solid food for a determined period of time. People who undertake extended fasts will use this form, even adding nutritional supplements to help sustain them for the duration.

One time, I was on a 21-day fast with Mike Bickle and some others. It was about day 17 or so, pretty far into the fast, when I heard the Holy Spirit whisper to me, "you must be careful because your electrolytes are out of balance."

I said, "My electro-whats? What in the world is an electrolyte?" I didn't know if I was supposed to rebuke the devil, rebuke my electrolytes, or what. So I went and looked up what it meant, and then I got myself some Gatorade to restore my electrolyte balance. I was like an athlete who needed to do that in order to keep training or competing. So I learned something practical about fasting in that season.

In the 21st century, there are several additional types of fasts that we can consider. These aren't in the Bible because these elements were not a part of the life of the Jews or the early Church:

- Fasting entertainment (movies, plays, perform-ances, videos, television, radio, video games, sec-ular dancing, etc.)

- Fasting athletic events (professional sports, non-professional athletic events, athletic recreation, etc.)

- Fasting reading material (books, even Christian books, magazines, newspapers, other news media, etc.)

- Fasting computers (internet activity, e-mail, games, etc.)

Restricting these things could be considered a valid fast. They are as much a part of our daily lives as food and drink.

In addition to the above, other forms of fasting can include restrictions on the following:

- Fasting speech (phone calls, conversations, limit-ing topics or amount of talking, special vows of silence, etc.)

- Fasting clothing (avoiding certain types and styles of clothing—or wearing only specific types of clothing, etc.)

- Fasting sleep (prayer watches at certain hours, early-morning prayer, all-night prayer vigils, etc.)

- Fasting social functions (limiting outside engagements, conferences, seminars, and even ordinary Church activities in order to spend time alone with God)

- Fasting work (taking hours or days off from secular work or even ministry engagements to seek God's face)

- Fasting sexual relations (this one is in the Bible):

The wife does not have authority over her own body, but the husband does. And likewise the husband does not have authority over his own body, but the wife does. Do not deprive one another except with consent for a time, that you may give yourselves to fasting and prayer; and come together again so that Satan does not tempt you because of your lack of self-control (1 Corinthians 7:4-5 NKJV).

FEATURES OF FASTING

It should go without saying, but I'll say it anyway—the primary activity that should accompany fasting is *prayer*. Fasting and prayer always go together:

So we fasted and sought our God concerning this matter, and He listened to our entreaty (Ezra 8:23).

When I heard these words, I sat down and wept and mourned for days; and I was fasting and praying before the God of heaven (Nehemiah 1:4).

Yet when they were ill, I put on sackcloth and humbled myself with fasting (Psalm 35:13 NIV).

So I turned to the Lord God and pleaded with Him in prayer and petition, in fasting, and in sackcloth and ashes (Daniel 9:3 NIV).

They said to him, "John's disciples often fast and pray, and so do the disciples of the Pharisees, but Yours go on eating and drinking." Jesus answered, "Can you make the guests of the bridegroom fast while He is with them? But the time will come when the bridegroom will be taken from them; in those days they will fast" (Luke 5:33-35 NIV).

Along with prayer, or as a type of prayer, *worship* plays a big part in any fast that has been ordained by God. So does *confession of sin*. (See Nehemiah 9:1-3 for an example of both; see also 1 Samuel 7:6.) After all, the sacrifices of fasting imply *humility*, and this turns out to be one of the most valuable outcomes of the discipline. Take a look at how often fasting and humility go together in the Bible; read Deuteronomy 9:18, Psalm 35:13, Psalm 69:10, and First Kings 21:27. Humility means more than feeling low. Often it includes outright *mourning* and *weeping*. "'Now, therefore,' says the Lord, 'Turn to Me with all your heart, with fasting, with weeping, and with mourning'" (Joel 2:12 NKJV). (See also Second Samuel 1:12, Esther 4:3, Nehemiah 1:4, and Ezra 10:6.)

One last accompaniment to the discipline of fasting is *reading the Scriptures*. For examples, look especially at Nehemiah 9:1-3 and also at Jeremiah 36:1-10.

Ten Biblical Fasts

I personally am indebted to Elmer L. Towns for the descriptions of the first nine of these Bible-inspired fasts. They are based on his book, *Fasting for Spiritual Breakthrough: A Guide to Nine Biblical Fasts*.[5] I adapted this teaching in my book, *The Lost Art of Practicing His Presence*, adding some of my own understandings.[6]

The Disciple's Fast

You will remember the dramatic story that Matthew told about the boy who the disciples could not set free from over-powering demonic control (see Matt. 17:14-21). In many translations, you will find this verse: "This kind [of spirit] does not go out except by prayer and fasting" (Matt. 17:21 NKJV). Jesus was implying that the disciples might have been successful—if they had fasted before they prayed.

In the Church today, modern disciples could employ fasting much more often than they do in order to "loose the bonds of wickedness" (Isa. 58:6 NKJV), thereby achieving victory over besetting sins and persistent, unhealed conditions.

The Ezra Fast

Ezra was the priest who had been given permission by the king of Persia to restore the Law of Moses as the Jews rebuilt Jerusalem. As they journeyed, their enemies came against them. Ezra had already obtained generous favors from the king, and he was reluctant to request the protection of the Persian army when he had expressed such definite assurance to the king that his God would protect them:

> *Then I proclaimed a fast there at the river of Ahava, that we might humble ourselves before our God, to seek from Him the right way for us and our little ones and all our possessions. For I was ashamed to request of the king an escort of soldiers and horsemen to help us against the enemy on the road, because we had spoken to the king, saying, "The hand of our God is upon all those for good who seek Him, but His power and His wrath are against all those who forsake Him." So we fasted and entreated our*

God for this, and He answered our prayer (Ezra 8:21-23 NKJV).

We can call it an Ezra fast when we fast for solutions to problems, inviting God to overcome obstacles and furnish protection so that we can complete a task or a journey successfully.

The Samuel Fast

The ark of the Lord had been captured by the Philistines, and then it had been returned to Kiriath-jearim, where it had remained for 20 long years. When Samuel urged the people to reform their ways and to eliminate the sins that had allowed the ark to be captured and held, he and the people "gathered to Mizpah, and drew water and poured it out before the Lord, and fasted on that day and said there, 'We have sinned against the Lord...'" (1 Sam. 7:6).

Their "Samuel fast," like ours, represented a strong plea to God for revival of past glory and relief from sin, for a breaking off of the kingdom of darkness and a breaking in of the Kingdom of God's glory.

The Widow's Fast

The purpose of the widow's fast is found in Isaiah 58, where we can find so many fast-produced blessings listed: The purpose is "to share your bread with the hungry" and to "bring to your house the poor" (Isa. 58:7 NKJV). You will remember the story of Elijah going to the home of the widow of Zarephath in the time of drought and famine. She was destitute, nearly starving, and she was preparing a final meal for herself and her son. Elijah's presence resulted in miraculous, sustained provision: "...She and he and her household ate for many days. The bin of flour was not used up, nor did the jar of oil run dry, according to the word of the Lord which He spoke by Elijah" (1 Kings 17:15-16 NKJV). In the same way today, we can present ourselves to the Lord in prayer and fasting, asking Him to relieve hunger.

The Elijah Fast

After Elijah prevailed over the prophets of Baal and also ushered in the return of rain to the drought-stricken land with his prayers, he had to run into the wilderness for his life. Jezebel had heard about what had happened to the prophets of Baal, and she wanted to kill him. All alone, he was destitute and desolate. God sent an angel to feed him, and while the text says nothing specifically about fasting, it does say that Elijah ate nothing more for 40 days:

> But he himself went a day's journey into the wilderness....The angel of the Lord came again a second time and touched him and said, "Arise, eat, because the journey is too great for you." So he arose and ate and drank, and went in the strength of that food forty days and forty nights... (1 Kings 19:4,7-8 NKJV).

At the end of that time, Elijah was able to resume his ministry. Today we undertake an "Elijah fast" in order "to break every yoke" (Isa. 58:6) of emotional and mental anguish, in particular, the aggressive religious spirit known as the "Jezebel spirit." Our desire is to ask God to control our lives and the lives of others instead of allowing them to be controlled by emotional or mental problems.

The Saint Paul Fast

The background for this fast is the story of how Saul of Tarsus,

...who became known as Paul after his conversion to Christ, was struck blind by the Lord in his act of persecuting Christians. Not only was he without literal sight, but he also had no clue about what direction his life was to take in the future. After going without food and praying for three days, Paul was visited by the Christian Ananias, and both his eyesight and his vision of the future were restored.[7]

During the time that he was blind, Paul went without food or drink for three days (see Acts 9:9). His fast, therefore, becomes a model for us when we want to allow God's light to penetrate our blindness, bringing us God's guidance as we make important decisions.

The Daniel Fast

Whenever we talk about partial fasts, we refer to the request of Daniel and his three friends who were being groomed for leadership in Babylon but who did not want to defile themselves with rich pagan foods. In compliance with their request, their steward allowed them to have only vegetables for their meals, after which they were remarkably healthier than their counterparts who had accepted the rich food. Where the Daniel fast is concerned, the two key verses of this account are verses 8 and 15 of the first chapter:

> *Daniel resolved not to defile himself with the royal food and wine, and he asked the chief official for permission not to defile himself this way....At the end of the ten days they looked healthier and better nourished than any of the young men who ate the royal food (Daniel 1:8,15 NIV).*

The purpose of a Daniel fast today is to regain and maintain health or to obtain healing. We read in Isaiah 58:6,8: "Is this not the fast that I have chosen?...Then...your healing shall spring forth speedily" (NKJV).

The Esther Fast

I have already mentioned Esther's fast, which involves abstaining from both food and water for three days in a desperate effort to stave off an enemy attack. The specific references to her fast and its results are found in the fourth and fifth chapters of the Book of Esther. When we undertake an Esther fast today, we are beseeching for the glory of the Lord to protect us from the evil one (see Isa. 58:8).

Our own ministry calls for three days of prayer with fasting during the season of Purim each year. This emphasis comes from our understanding of the book of Esther, when prayer with fasting saved the entire Jewish people from annihilation. The enemy, Haman, was hanged on his own gallows, and Queen Esther and her court were honored for their humble and bold acts of intervention.

In a similar way, Encounters Network and Prayer Storm call the modern-day Esther—the Bride and Body of Christ—to seek the Lord each year during the three days of the Feast of Purim for intervention on behalf of God's purposes for Israel and the Jewish people worldwide. We believe that we Gentile believers should carry the Jewish people on our hearts before the Lord of Hosts, and we want to do our part through what we call The Cry. See Appendix B in the back of this book for the dates of The Cry and how you can participate.

The John the Baptist Fast

John the Baptist came to announce Jesus' arrival; he was Jesus' "forerunner." As a Nazarite from birth (see Luke 1:15), he was not allowed to drink wine or strong drink, which of course is a form of fasting. His disciples fasted also (see Matt. 9:14; Mark 2:18; Luke 5:33). Therefore, undertaking a John the Baptist fast means abstaining from some degree of sustenance with the goal of obtaining favor for our testimony, influence, or witness before others. Inevitably, one of the results of such a fast will be to increase a person's holiness before God. The actual details of what the person abstains from are not as important as the goal of the fast.

The Bridegroom Fast

In our day, we have added one more distinct kind of fast, the Bridegroom fast. Those who undertake the Bridegroom fast are motivated, like Jesus' disciples, by a "lovesick heart":

> *Jesus said to them, "Can the friends of the bridegroom mourn as long as the bridegroom is with them? But the days will come when the bridegroom will be taken away from them, and then they will fast"* (Matthew 9:15 NKJV).

Mike Bickle, founder and director of the International House of Prayer in Kansas City and a strong advocate of the Bridegroom fast and of an overall "fasted lifestyle," states that fasting is directly related to experiencing the presence of the Bridegroom Jesus.[8] In other words, the highest purpose for this discipline is to develop in us a greater spiritual capacity for intimacy (as part of the Bride of Christ, the Church) with our Bridegroom.

The Book of Joel paints us a picture of the time of the last days, during which seeking God's face with fasting precedes the great latter-rain outpouring and a worldwide display of God's glory (see Joel 2:12,23,30-32).

Mike Bickle hosts a monthly Global Bridegroom Fast (GBF), which occurs on the first Monday, Tuesday, and Wednesday of each month, with seven days in December, for a total of 40 days of deliberate prayer and fasting each year.[9] This is a kind of a global solemn assembly that includes believers from all around the world. It is my hope that the Prayer Storm team will participate in this endeavor as the Lord gives them grace to do so. This is not so much an event as it is a total lifestyle, and the fasting will continue until the Lord Jesus' Second Coming.

The goals of the Global Bridegroom Fast overlap with our Prayer Storm goals:

- *Fullness of the Holy Spirit and unity throughout the Church* (John 14:12; 17:2-23): Spiritual breakthroughs in the worldwide Church with unprecedented unity, purity and power

- *The Great Harvest* (Matt. 24:14): Over one billion souls converted by the power of God

- *Youth revival movement* (Mal. 4:6): Worldwide revival especially among the poor of the earth

- *Revival to Israel* (Rom. 9-11): Fulfillment of all the prophetic promises to national Israel

- *Houses of prayer* (Isa. 62:6-7): The release of "grace for fasting" with worship and prayer to establish 24/7 houses of prayer in the cities of the earth, including Israel

- *Wealth of the nations* (Hag. 2:7-9): Release of finances for the Great Harvest, the prayer movement, and the poor

- *The "wall of fire"* (Zech. 2:5): Divine protection of all that is birthed through prayer[10]

BLESSINGS PROMISED FROM FASTING WITH PRAYER

It is time to restore the lost art of fasting as a weapon of spiritual warfare for such a time as this. Will you join with me and thousands of others as we sacrifice the temporary pleasures of this life for the eternal pleasures of His Kingdom? It is worth the cost! On a personal level, you can expect that living a fasted lifestyle will make it possible for you to (1) receive more revelation of the beauty of our marvelous God as you pour over His Word; (2) receive a greater measure of revelation in an accelerated way; (3) experience a speeded-up process of getting rid of hard-heartedness, old strongholds, and old mindsets; and (4) experience God's love for you and your love for Him as never before.

So if you want to experience more of Jesus in a deeper way, start fasting with a focus on Jesus as the Bridegroom. The Holy Spirit gives grace and revelation to His people who are not afraid to cry out for it. And your fast—which is like God's *feast* for His Bride—will mature you so that you can enter into intimacy with your Bridegroom. The revelation you will receive will touch you at a deeper level. You will be able to assume your true identity in Christ and be fully prepared for His return.

Arthur Wallis, the British pastor who wrote the classic book, *God's Chosen Fast,* put it this way:

> Before the Bridegroom left them He promised that He would come again to receive them to Himself. The Church still awaits the midnight cry, 'Behold, the bridegroom! Come out to meet him' (Matt. 25.6). It is this age of the Church that is the period of the absent Bridegroom. It is this age of the Church to which our Master referred when He said, "*Then* they will fast."

These words of Jesus were prophetic. The first Christians fulfilled them, and so have many saintly men and women of succeeding generations. Where are those who fulfil them today? Alas, they are few and far between, the exception rather than the rule, to the great loss of the Church.

A new generation, however, is arising. There is concern in the hearts of many for the recovery of apostolic power. But how can we recover apostolic power while neglecting apostolic practice? How can we expect the power to flow if we do not prepare the channels? Fasting is a God-appointed means for the flowing of His grace and power that we can afford to neglect no longer.

The fast of this age is not merely an act of mourning for Christ's absence, but an act of preparation for His return. May those prophetic words, '"Then will they fast"', be finally fulfilled in this generation. It will be a fasting and praying Church that will hear the thrilling cry, 'Behold, the Bridegroom!' Tears shall then be wiped away, and *the fast* be followed by *the feast* at the marriage supper of the Lamb.[11]

You may be able already to add your endorsement to mine and to many others'—God surely bestows His blessings on those who fast and pray. Here are a number of the blessings that you can expect to receive when you fast and pray, listed under the specific Scripture passages where the promises appear:

Isaiah 58:6-12

Blessings include:

• Loosing the bands of wickedness

- Undoing heavy burdens
- Setting the oppressed free
- Breaking the yoke of bondage
- Attaining health
- Maintaining righteousness
- Seeing the glory of the Lord
- Receiving guidance from the Lord continually
- Having one's soul satisfied, even in times of spiritual drought
- Achieving fruitfulness and productivity
- Enhancing the ministry of reconciliation

First Corinthians 9:27

Fasting disciplines our bodies, subdues our flesh, and allows our spirits to be strengthened by God's grace and peace. "I discipline my body and bring it into subjection, lest, when I have preached to others, I myself should become disqualified" (1 Cor. 9:27 NKJV).

Matthew 17:21

Fasting is a strong tool that gives believers God's manifested power against the works of darkness. "This kind [of spirit] does not go out except by prayer and fasting" (Matt. 17:21).

Acts 13:1-3

In Antioch, fasting with prayer was received by the Lord as acceptable ministry to Him:

In the church at Antioch there were prophets and teachers: Barnabas, Simeon called Niger, Lucius of Cyrene, Manaen (who had been brought up with Herod the tetrarch) and Saul. While they were worshiping the Lord and fasting, the Holy Spirit said, "Set apart for me Barnabas and Saul for the work to which I have called them." So after they had fasted and prayed, they placed their hands on them and sent them off (Acts 13:1-3 NIV).

I like what Lou Engle, the founder of The Call, says: "We have taught our people to feast and pray. Now it is time to teach our people to fast and pray."[12]

Father, we submit our wills to Your desires. We declare that it is an honor to co-labor with You for Your divine intervention in the earth. Reveal this to each of us as the marvelous privilege that it is. Give us the grace we surely need to fast and to pray. Lead us into all of the applications that You would have us make in these days, as individuals and as groups of people who love You. Thank You for making it possible for us to draw closer to You, even as You draw closer to us. Amen.

I Need Thee Every Hour

I need Thee every hour, most gracious Lord;
No tender voice like Thine can peace afford.

(Refrain) *I need Thee, O I need Thee;*
Every hour I need Thee;
O bless me now, my Savior,
I come to Thee.

I need Thee every hour, stay Thou nearby;
Temptations lose their power when Thou art nigh.

I need Thee every hour, in joy or pain;
Come quickly and abide, or life is in vain.

I need Thee every hour; teach me Thy will;
And Thy rich promises in me fulfill.

I need Thee every hour, most Holy One;
O make me Thine indeed, Thou blessèd Son.[1]

Chapter 6

Soaking in His Presence

Come to Me, all who are weary and heavy-laden, and I will give you rest. Take My yoke upon you and learn from Me, for I am gentle and humble in heart, and you will find rest for your souls. For My yoke is easy and My burden is light (Matthew 11:28-30).

In the midst of birthing and maintaining your Prayer Storm, don't neglect your personal devotional intimacy with Jesus. If you do, you will run out of grace for your assignments. You will not be able to keep your "machine" going. You know how it is with machinery. You have to keep it oiled, or it just cranks dry and stops. It's the same with your spiritual life; you have to keep the oil of intimacy flowing and covering all the parts of your life. First Thessalonians 5:17 reminds us to "pray without ceasing." That means that our prayer machinery needs to be in good working order all the time.

Intercession is hard work without the grace of God. In fact, without the pervasive, soaking oil of the presence of Jesus' Spirit, prayer and intercession just plain shut down. We can't afford to let that happen! We're living in the endtimes, and we need to be like the wise virgins in Jesus' parable:

Then the kingdom of heaven shall be likened to ten virgins who took their lamps and went out to meet the bridegroom. Now five of them were wise, and five were foolish. Those who were foolish took their lamps and took no oil with them, but the wise took oil in their vessels with their lamps. But while the bridegroom was delayed, they all slumbered and slept. And at midnight a cry was heard: "Behold, the bridegroom is coming; go out to meet Him!" Then all those virgins arose and trimmed their lamps. And the foolish said to the wise, "Give us some of your oil, for our lamps are going out." But the wise answered, saying, "No, lest there should not be enough for us and you; but go rather to those who sell, and buy for yourselves." And while they went to buy, the bridegroom came, and those who were ready went in with Him to the wedding; and the door was shut.

Afterward the other virgins came also, saying, "Lord, Lord, open to us!" But He answered and said, "Assuredly, I say to you, I do not know you." Watch therefore, for you know neither the day nor the hour in which the Son of Man is coming (Matthew 25:1-13 NKJV).

This parable is supposed to be a wake-up call to the Church. All ten of the virgins represent born-again believers. Each one had a knowledge of the Bridegroom, and each one carried a lamp, which is the same as having a ministry. (See Matthew 5:15; Revelation 1:20; 2:5; 11:3-6; Zechariah 4:2; Isaiah 62:1; John 5:35.) Paul pointed out how God views the Church as a virgin: "I am jealous for you with a godly jealousy. I promised you to one husband, to Christ, so that I might present you as a pure virgin to Him" (2 Cor. 11:2 NIV). Taken separately or together, we're each (all) viewed as virgins.

So you need to understand that the foolish virgins are not being labeled as wicked, sinful, lazy, fearful, or even cursed. They simply did not think ahead or make the effort to get the oil that they needed. They didn't lose their "fire insurance," their salvation. It's the same with us. The Church is full of the redeemed. All of us have been bought with Jesus' blood. But not everybody in the Church ends up fulfilling his or her personal destiny. Not everybody ends up in the center circle at the end of the age.

All of the virgins together came out to meet the Bridegroom. They left their ordinary occupations and joined together in a group that was going to meet Him. The oil that some of them neglected to obtain is, of course, the same as our relationship with the Holy Spirit. They failed to nurture that relationship. Somehow, they were caught up in so many other things that they just didn't properly manage their devotional life. The rat race kept them too distracted. But at the midnight hour of history, they were left in the dust. The "forerunners," the wise virgins, raised the cry, "The Bridegroom is coming!" and they lit their lamps and rushed off to greet Him. Before the ones whose lamps had burned out could do anything to stop it, the door was shut.

Jesus' upcoming arrival has serious consequences. We must not only expect Him and even go out to meet Him, but we must also make the necessary effort to be prepared to meet Him. We will all go through "slumber," because our lives are lived in the context of natural processes. We can't keep our eyes open every minute. But when that final wake-up call comes, how many of us will have oil already in our lamps? Will we open our eyes and see the flame in the lamp guttering down as the last of our diminished fuel is consumed? Will our opportunity and ability to minister be almost finished?

It will be too late then to obtain some oil from somebody else. You won't have time to go to another conference or read another book or listen to another CD. *Spiritual preparedness is not transferable. Intimacy with Jesus cannot be gained by impartation.*

Each of us must engage in the God-ordained process of acquiring oil for ourselves. Why? God is jealous for each of us.

You have to maintain a devotional life with God. You have to commune with Him by yourself and for yourself. Rick Joyner has said many times, "You're as close to God as you want to be." To change the metaphor from oil for a minute, each of us needs to heed the words of Jesus in Revelation: "I advise you to buy from Me gold refined by fire so that you may become rich, and white garments so that you may clothe yourself, and that the shame of your nakedness will not be revealed; and eye salve to anoint your eyes so that you may see" (Rev. 3:18).

The saddest thing is that many of us, like the foolish virgins, will miss out on future opportunities to be used in our fullest capacity. The Bridegroom will not recognize some of us as those who are "engaged" to Him. It is absolutely vital that we obtain and maintain the oil in our lamps, the oil of intimacy with our Bridegroom. We need to get it now and to keep refilling our lamps whenever we can.

GETTING THE OIL

We can't use the excuse that Jesus didn't tell us about this ahead of time. One of His primary emphases was on "watching," not as much in a military or protective sense as in the sense of keeping Him company, staying awake with Him, and developing a deep and sustained relationship with Him, largely so that we will be ready and quick to move when necessary.

When I was preparing my first book, *The Lost Art of Intercession*, I did a comparative study in all four Gospel accounts of what Jesus said would happen in the last days, the endtimes, and specifically what response He was looking for in His people. I found that one word was used often in all four accounts.

In fact, three times more often than any other response, Jesus wanted to see *watching*. He wanted people to be awake and alert in their spirits.

Here is what He said:

> *But of that day and hour no one knows, not even the angels in heaven, nor the Son, but only the Father. Take heed, watch and pray; for you do not know when the time is…. Watch therefore, for you do not know when the master of the house is coming—in the evening, at midnight, at the crowing of the rooster, or in the morning—lest, coming suddenly, he find you sleeping. And what I say to you, I say to all: Watch!* (Mark 13:32-33;35-37 NKJV).

Jesus warned His followers to "watch out that the light in you is not darkness" (Luke 11:35). And He even warned them to watch for the right bridegroom: "Watch out that you are not deceived. For many will come in My name, claiming, 'I am He,' and, 'The time is near.' Do not follow them" (Luke 21:8 NIV).

Remember what He said in the Garden of Gethsemane, right before He was arrested and crucified. Jesus wanted His disciples to be ready for what was about to happen, and He also craved the comfort of knowing that He was not entirely alone: "Then He returned to His disciples and found them sleeping. 'Could you men not keep watch with Me for one hour?' He asked Peter" (Matt. 26:40 NIV).

Watching, you see, although it seems impractical to many, is the only way to receive the preparation, strength, and supernatural courage needed to face whatever is coming. Watching also establishes a lifestyle of encountering Jesus. Watching in the Spirit hinders satan from stealing our inheritance (see John 10:10). Since our primary inheritance is our heart-connection with Jesus, protecting that connection means that we have also protected the rest of our inheritance.

In other words, we need to spend *being*-time with Jesus more than we need to spend *doing*-time with Him. The amazing thing about this is that our "doing" becomes more effective simply because we have spent time at His feet. When we come to Him, we find rest for our souls. We find oil for our lamps. We find grace for the tasks ahead.

You see, Prayer Storm is not just about crisis intervention, it's about watching in the sense of maintaining an "oiled heart." It's about having a heart that's ready to respond instantly when it hears the Master's voice.

SOAKING IN HIS PRESENCE

You hear a lot these days in the Church about "soaking." Some people object to it, because that term is not in the Bible. (Of course, a lot of things we do are not directly in the Bible. Sunday school isn't. Electric guitar music isn't.) But the soaking concept is there—it's all over the place. It's in almost every book of the Bible, even in First Samuel. You can see it in this familiar story:

Now the boy Samuel was ministering to the Lord before Eli. And word from the Lord was rare in those days, visions were infrequent. It happened at that time as Eli was lying down in his place (now his eyesight had begun to grow dim and he could not see well), and the lamp of God had not yet gone out, and Samuel was lying down in the temple of the Lord where the ark of God was, that the Lord called Samuel; and he said, "Here I am." Then he ran to Eli and said, "Here I am, for you called me." But he said, "I did not call, lie down again." So he went and lay down. The Lord

*called yet again, "Samuel!" So Samuel arose and went to
Eli and said, "Here I am, for you called me." But he
answered, "I did not call, my son, lie down again"*
(1 Samuel 3:1-6).

Where did young Samuel lie down? Where did he sleep?
He "was lying down in the temple of the Lord where the ark of
God was." Little Samuel had been brought to the old priest Eli
by his mother Hannah, and he lived there in the temple, ministering to the Lord and learning about God. At night, he lay
down to rest near the ark itself.

And when the voice of the Lord was released, but Samuel
couldn't yet discern that it was God's voice, what did Eli tell
him to do? He told him to go lie down there again. He didn't
keep him wherever he was sleeping, and he didn't send him
somewhere else to do something. In essence, Eli told Samuel to
go and soak up some more of God's presence so that he would
recognize the voice of God when he heard it.

This is instructive for us. Like Samuel, we need to spend
time resting in God's presence, going back again and again,
falling in love with God all over again. We can be *changed*, not
just temporarily stirred up, by returning to our first love (or by
finding that first love if we've never tasted it before). We can
learn to recognize His voice, and we can experience personal
revival. Out of that renewal, we can obey the voice of God as we
minister.

When you seek Him, you will find Him (see Matt. 7:7).
Imagine for a moment that you could spend a day with Jesus,
just the two of you. If that's too much time to imagine spending
with Him, imagine spending only an hour with Him. Imagine
that it's right now, right this minute—just you and the lover of
your soul. Just *be*.

Go ahead, soak in His presence. If it helps to put on a quiet worship CD, feel free to do that. You can find Him in ever so many ways. One of my favorite ways is hiking alone in the woods. When I was growing up, it was walking on the railroads tracks outside my parents' house in rural Missouri. You can find Him in the love letters (the Bible) that He wrote for you to read. You can see Him in the flowers that are blooming and in the creation that's groaning around you. You can see Him in the Body of Christ. But draw closer still. Yes, draw closer to His loving heart. While going through my cancer battles, I would simply put on some great "healing, soaking music" and rest in the presence of the Lord right in my bed. I found Him waiting to meet me every time.

Get alone with God the Father, God the Son, and God the Holy Spirit. Rest around the ark, like Samuel did. Take a "selah" pause from the hectic pace of this life. Rest. Wait. Repose. Reflect on the One who loves you more than you love yourself. Worship. Listen. Respond.

Get still before Him in order to commune with Him. (Read Psalm 46:10; Second Samuel 7:18; Revelation 3:20; and Habakkuk 2:20.)

Draw near to His heart. (Read James 4:8; Psalm 42:1-2; Isaiah 55:1-3,6; Psalm 65:4; Psalm 73:28; Psalm 84:1-4,10; and Hebrews 10:22.)

Seek His face. Seek His face, not His intervention. Seek God for God's sake. If you want to become an effective part of the Prayer Storm team, I encourage you to *engage* yourself with the Lord, in order to be able to engage yourself in the work of praying. (Read Matthew 7:7-8; Psalm 27:4,8; Psalm 63:1-8; Hebrews 11:6; and Jeremiah 29:11-14.)

Just spend time in His presence. Become an Exodus-33-aholic like Moses. (Read Exodus 33:14-15; Psalm 16:11; Psalm 89:15; Isaiah 29:13; Isaiah 63:9; Lamentations 2:19; and Jude 24- 25.)

Keep that oil replenished. Keep your lamp trimmed and ready. Get to know God. Address Him by one of His many names. You can find over a hundred of them in His Word. Sometimes one of them will capture your heart. Stay with it a while, even for the rest of the day.

I remember one time when I landed on "Friend of Sinners," and the Holy Spirit just fastened it onto my heart and unfolded it to me. You can get to know God—and you can minister His presence to others—when you address Him by various names and learn to know Him through His Word. (See Matthew 11:29; Jeremiah 9:23-24; and Philippians 3:8,10.)

If you count all things as loss in comparison to knowing Him, that's getting oil in your lamp. (Read Philippians 3:7-8; First Chronicles 21:23; and Second Samuel 24:24.) It's also a great trade!

Allow yourself to be overwhelmed by the amazing Person you are speaking with. You are talking *with* Him, not merely *to* Him; He is speaking back to you. The God of the Universe likes to hear your voice. (Read Romans 5:5; Psalm 143:8,10; Isaiah 54:10; Lamentations 3:22-25; John 17:23b; and Romans 8:35-39.)

GATHER STRENGTH IN THE EYE OF THE STORM

You'll be no more effective as an intercessor in Prayer Storm than you are in your private "watching and waiting" times with the Lord. You have the lamp in your hand already—God gave it to you when you were saved. Now it's time to gather the lamp-oil and keep it fresh.

It's like being in the eye of the hurricane, where you can re-gather your strength and your resources for the next onslaught. Your strength is in Him. Sit, rest, sleep right at His feet. Gather strength from being in His presence. The oil of His presence will soothe your wounds and aching muscles. It will lubricate your joints and limber up your mental processes. It will tender-ize your heart. Seek Him. Soak in Him. Let Him prepare you for what's next. Learn to let go!

Father, I present myself before You in Jesus' great name. I come as an intercessor, but this time all I want is more of You. Let my words be pleasing to You. Awaken my soul and spirit to hear Your voice. I love you, and I want to love you more. I want to be like young Samuel and learn to rest around the ark. I want to soak in Your presence. Draw me close to You. Let me hear Your heart beat. Pull my deepest heartstrings. I want to know Your voice and mirror Your ways. I choose Your ways over mine. Give me oil in my lamp, and grace me to be a wise attendant in these days that I live in. I come to You with expectancy and joy. Amen!

To God Be the Glory

To God be the glory, great things He has done;
So loved He the world that He gave us His Son,
Who yielded His life an atonement for sin,
And opened the life gate that all may go in.

(Refrain) *Praise the Lord, praise the Lord,*
Let the earth hear His voice!
Praise the Lord, praise the Lord,
Let the people rejoice!
O come to the Father, through Jesus the Son,
And give Him the glory, great things He has done.

O perfect redemption, the purchase of blood,
To every believer the promise of God;
The vilest offender who truly believes,
That moment from Jesus a pardon receives.

Great things He has taught us, great things He has done,
And great our rejoicing through Jesus the Son;
But purer, and higher, and greater will be
Our wonder, our transport, when Jesus we see.[1]

Chapter 7

TAPPING THE POWER OF HIGH PRAISE

Then Jonah prayed to the Lord his God from the fish's belly. And he said: "I cried out to the Lord because of my affliction, and He answered me....All Your billows and Your waves passed over me. Then I said, 'I have been cast out of Your sight; yet I will look again toward Your holy temple.' The waters surrounded me, even to my soul; the deep closed around me; weeds were wrapped around my head....When my soul fainted within me, I remembered the Lord; and my prayer went up to You, into Your holy temple....I will sacrifice to You with the voice of thanksgiving; I will pay what I have vowed. Salvation is of the Lord" (Jonah 2:1,3-5,7,9 NKJV).

I love movies. And one movie that I would really like to see produced is a movie about Jonah. I would like it to be the most realistic rendition possible of the story that we've been reading since we were children. I can just see it: fast-forward through the first part, and then there old Jonah would be in the belly of the sea monster, seaweed wrapped around his head, marinating in all kinds of interesting juices, about as low as a man can get.

I want to see the part where Jonah is standing (or sitting, or rolling around) in the middle of the whale (or sea monster or Behemoth or whatever he/she/it was), and Jonah gets so desperate that he starts praising the Lord because, well, what else could he do? I want to see the scene where he starts praising God, and then the sea monster gets a crazy look in one eye that means, "I have an idea. I think I will surface. Now." And from way down in the depths of the sea, as Jonah keeps on praising, the spiritual atmosphere keeps changing from about as low as it can get to something much higher as the creature swims up and up.

And when it gets to the surface, the creature swims to the shore. And there God speaks to it and says something like, "Hey, Dude, I got a ministry for you. How would you like to throw this guy up? How would you like being an instrument of deliverance?" And uurrpp, out comes Jonah. Now he's *really* a sight—covered not only in the remnants of the seaweed, but also dripping with green bile and with a nice, new, gritty breading of sand. So then he picks himself up and takes himself straight to Ninevah (not planning to disobey this time, no sir!). And when he points his bony finger at the people and tells them to repent, what do you think will happen? I mean, they'll probably run into each other trying to get away from this scary guy. But they *will* repent. The whole place will repent. You and I will repent too, even before we finish our popcorn!

PRAISE IS A SPIRITUAL WEAPON

The way I see it, the story of Jonah illustrates this essential spiritual truth, among others: praising God is a spiritual weapon. When Paul and Silas began to praise God in the middle of the night in the prison, the doors were opened, and their bonds fell off (see Acts 16:25-26). When we begin to praise the Lord in the midst of a terrible situation, God's salvation and deliverance begin to enter in (see Ps. 50:23).

If nothing else, praise is a way to silence the devil. Praise is a childlike expression of faith in a world where complicated minds tend to over-analyze circumstances and can see no reason for praising God. "Out of the mouth of babes and nursing infants You have ordained strength, because of Your enemies, that You may silence the enemy and the avenger" (Ps. 8:2 NKJV).

Praise opens the way into Christ's victory, as evidenced by verse after verse in the Bible and by the personal experience of many people over the centuries. (See Psalm 106:47; Colossians 2:15; and Second Corinthians 2:14.)

PRAISE IS A SACRIFICE

Praising the Lord is not always easy. (I don't think it was easy at all for Jonah.) According to Jeremiah 33:11, praise is a sacrifice, and it costs us something. We do not necessarily praise God because we feel like doing it. However, we praise Him because of what He has already done for us. Praise is the voice of the earthly Bride offering a "thank offering" to her heavenly Bridegroom.

PRAISE IS A GARMENT OF THE SPIRIT

According to Isaiah 61:1-3, the Gospel of praise can release us from the spirit of heaviness, which weighs us down like a gloomy cloak, and it can clothe us in a light, glorious, and beautiful garment:

The Spirit of the Lord God is upon me, because the Lord has anointed me to bring good news to the afflicted; He has sent me to bind up the brokenhearted, to proclaim liberty to captives and freedom to prisoners; to proclaim the favorable year of the Lord and the day of vengeance of our God; to comfort all who mourn, to grant those who mourn in Zion, giving them a garland instead of ashes, the oil of gladness instead of mourning, the mantle of praise instead of a spirit of fainting so they will be called oaks of righteousness, the planting of the Lord, that He may be glorified (Isaiah 61:1-3).

PRAISE IS THE WAY INTO GOD'S PRESENCE

It's like a giant gateway. All you have to do is walk through it with praises on your lips. Isaiah depicts it this way: "You will call your walls Salvation and your gates Praise" (Isa. 60:18b NIV). The Book of Psalms was written to usher worshippers through the gates of praise into God's Presence: "Enter His gates with thanksgiving and His courts with praise; give thanks to Him and praise His name" (Ps. 100:4 NIV).

As part of Prayer Storm, I want to see the gate of praise, the praise watch, established in every city, in every state, and in every part of this nation and the world. I want to join with you and others to keep the gate of praise inhabited with praises, releasing the King of Glory to enter.

PRAISE IS THE PLACE OF GOD'S RESIDENCE

Not only is praise the gate, it's the house! Praise is the place where God dwells. Nobody needs to be told that God's house must be holy. It's a holy and sanctified place. According to Psalm 22, God is holy, and He cannot dwell in an unholy place: "You are holy, enthroned in the praises of Israel" (Ps. 22:3 NKJV).

GOD'S BLESSING RELEASES PRAISE

When it comes to praising God to this degree, nobody can achieve it. We need the Holy Spirit within us to release the high praises of God and to put them on our tongues. The phrase *my glory rejoices* in Psalm 16:9 (NKJV) is interesting, because sometimes the Hebrew phrase *my glory* is used to refer to the human tongue. So some translations say it: "my tongue rejoices." In another psalm, God intervened in David's situation so that his tongue could be used to praise Him: "I will extol You, O Lord, for You have lifted me up, and have not let my enemies rejoice over me….Sing praise to the Lord, you His godly ones, and give thanks to His holy name…" (Psalm 30:1,4).

WORSHIP AND PRAISE TOGETHER

Worship and praise are like a happily married couple—not quite the same as each other, but inseparable and bearing a certain resemblance to each other. Worship is primarily an inner attitude that is exhibited through a person's posture. It means to bow down in submission before the awesome holiness of God. Worship is what's happening in Heaven all the time. It's what's portrayed in Isaiah 6:1-4, where we see four-winged seraphs—they use two of their wings to cover themselves, which portrays worship, and the other two wings to fly, which portrays service. They cry praise with their mouths, declaring, "Holy! Holy! Holy!" Worship is also what we see in the Book of Revelation:

> And when the living creatures give glory and honor and thanks to Him who sits on the throne, to Him who lives forever and ever, the twenty-four elders will fall down before Him who sits on the throne, and will worship Him who lives forever and ever, and will cast their crowns before the throne, saying, "Worthy are You, our Lord and our God, to receive glory and honor and power; for You created all things, and because of Your will they existed, and were created" (Revelation 4:9-11).

Thanksgiving and praise are what worshippers *do*. We thank and praise God for what He is doing right now and for what He has done in the past. We thank and praise Him for what He does for us and for what He has done for other people. We worship Him as our Creator and as the Creator of everything in the world around us. We open our mouths with words of praise, recounting God's deeds and His goodness. (See Psalm 48:1, which is just one of many verses that exemplify praise.)

Thanksgiving is directly commanded by God, according to Colossians 3:15-17 and First Thessalonians 5:16-18. In other words, giving thanks is related to being in God's will. Have you ever thought about it that way before? Do you want to be in God's will? Just start praising Him! "Rejoice always, pray without ceasing, in everything give thanks; for this is the will of God in Christ Jesus for you" (1 Thess. 5:16-18 NKJV).

Thanksgiving and praise are necessary to make other forms of prayer effective. They are like the railroad track that carries the payload of prayer. Paul urged the Philippians and the Colossians to "be anxious for nothing, but in everything by prayer and supplication with thanksgiving let your requests be made known to God" (Phil. 4:6) and to "devote yourselves to prayer, keeping alert in it with an attitude of thanksgiving" (Col. 4:2).

Thanksgiving, you see, is the key to releasing God's supernatural power. (See the story of the loaves and fishes in John 6, especially verses 11 and 23, and the story of the raising of Lazarus in John 11, especially verses 41-44.) Besides that, thanksgiving and praise set a seal on the blessings that we have already received, keeping them safe. (See the story of the ten lepers in Luke 17:12-19.)

When you combine it all—worship, thanksgiving, and praise—with the worship, thanksgiving, and praise of faithful believers throughout the earth, you become part of a great symphony of praise, an antiphonal call-and-response that rebounds from earth to Heaven and back. Because the Hebrews weren't as linear in their approach to things as the Greeks were or modern Western thinkers are, the Hebraic understanding of "the symphony of praise" does not separate praise from thanksgiving or thanksgiving from worship, and none of them are separated from prayer and intercession. In fact, even the methods of offering praiseful prayers or prayerful praises were not separated; sometimes they sang their petitions to God along with their praises.

So it's a little artificial to define and separate these elements, since they are intertwined together: praise, thanksgiving, worship, intercession, prayer. The foundational message is the same—*do it!*

THE WHEN, HOW, AND WHO OF PRAISE

When should we praise the Lord? That's easy to answer: we should praise the Lord at all times, continually, every day, forever and ever, and into eternity (see Ps. 34; 145:2). We're just getting warmed up!

How should we praise Him? That's easy to answer, too. We should praise the Lord with our whole hearts—wholeheartedly (see Ps. 111:1). We should praise Him intentionally and with skill and understanding (see Ps. 47:7). We should praise Him with uplifted hands, a joyful mouth, and all the physical expressions that go along with that (see Ps. 63:3-4; 1 Tim. 2:8-9). We can praise Him with dancing, demonstrations of worship, gratitude, and thankfulness (see Ps. 149:3; 150:4). Our prayers go up to the nostrils of God just as incense, and our uplifted hands are like the evening sacrifice to Him (see Ps. 141:2).

Who should praise the Lord? Everyone. Not just human beings. Not just believers. Everything that has breath, as a matter of fact. "Let everything that has breath praise the Lord. Praise the Lord!" (Ps. 150:6 NKJV). Keep in mind that high-tech recordings, as helpful and good as they are, do not have breath. High-tech worship doesn't breathe. No matter how wonderful the artists or the bands or how pure the sound, God never meant for any recording to be used as a substitute for our own personal praise coming out of our own mouths. Only the dead, who cannot breathe, absolutely cannot praise the Lord.

It is "the high praises of God in our mouths" that empower our prayers to the max. "Let the high praises of God be in their mouth, and a two-edged sword in their hand" (Ps. 149:6 KJV). We may not sound quite as professional as the praise from the recording companies, but there is something irreplaceable about learning to praise God for ourselves. There is something powerful in our praise, something that can shake the enemy camp. Praise is one of the highest expressions of spiritual warfare. Worship and thanksgiving can place demonic principalities in chains. In our praises, we simply declare that which is already written in the Word of God. We remind the enemy once more that "it is finished" (see John 19:30). The great war between Jesus Christ and satan, between good and evil, is finished. The Victor was determined at the cross. Once and for all, God disarmed all the satanic forces by the death and resurrection of His Son.

By praise and worship, we enforce and extend the victory already won at Calvary. This is the honor given to all of His godly ones!

Praise the Lord! Sing to the Lord a new song, and His praise in the congregation of the godly ones. Let Israel be glad in his Maker; let the sons of Zion rejoice in their King.

Let them praise His name with dancing; let them sing praises to Him with timbrel and lyre. For the Lord takes pleasure in His people; He will beautify the afflicted ones with salvation. Let the godly ones exult in glory; let them sing for joy on their beds. Let the high praises of God be in their mouth, and a two-edged sword in their hand, to execute vengeance on the nations and punishment on the peoples, to bind their kings with chains and their nobles with fetters of iron, to execute on them the judgment written; this is an honor for all His godly ones. Praise the Lord! (Psalm 149).

Intercessory Worship

I want to run through a number of things that intercessory worship—combining the worship of God's holiness and "watching"—can do. Here they are, for all of you Prayer Stormers:

1. Intercessory worship *enthrones* God.

2. Intercessory worship *encounters* God.

3. Intercessory worship *enlarges* God to us.

4. Intercessory worship *enjoys* God.

5. Intercessory worship *enlists* God to move.

6. Intercessory worship *excites* God.

We are privileged to be living in a time when songs of breakthrough are being sung. These aren't necessarily new lyrics set to new music, although they can be. Whether they are played with old instruments or new, these songs of breakthrough are *fresh*. They invigorate those who sing them and those who hear them. They help us touch God; they are songs of enthronement, songs of harvest, songs of the Spirit, songs of prophetic declaration and intercession.

When worshippers who have a forerunner anointing on them sing songs of breakthrough, they can help prepare the atmosphere and break open the heavens so that the Son of Glory can come down into our midst and be glorified. They begin to declare in song things that have not yet happened, and as the songs are sung, they become not only songs of exaltation to God but also a kind of heavenly download. The King is enthroned. The priest petitions. The prophet releases revelation. Then the King releases a decree, and the decree resonates in the hearts of those who are united with Him.

Our prayers break outside the walls of our place of worship. When we break outside the walls of the Church with our praises, we become like one of the Salvation Army bands of William and Catherine Booth who not only praised God inside the house but who also went out onto the streets. That's where satan gets crushed under the "army boots" of the Bride (see Rom. 16:20). We go into the house of worship to pick up the brilliant glory of God, which fills our hearts and glows on our skin and hair and radiates from our eyes, and then we turn around and release His Presence into the world around us.

We are supposed to get the Presence for a *purpose*, and we get it by means of worship, praise, and thanksgiving. Come on now—don't hold back! You do not have to get swallowed up by life's circumstances, as Jonah did, before you begin to praise the Lord. Start right now! Create a culture of His presence in your home, neighborhood, and yes, even your car (as dangerous as that might sound). Let's tap into the high power of praise and bind up the enemy's works for Jesus Christ's sake. Let's just praise the Lord!

Without further preliminaries, I want to begin praising you, Lord! I want to be an instrument in the symphony of praise that rises from the earth to Your throne. I want the sounds from my little piece of the earth to come into agreement with all the sounds of Heaven. I want You to mount up on my praises and on the praises of myriads of others, wearing Your royal crown. I am dependent upon You to help me love and praise You. I open my heart to you, and I let my faith rise to meet You. I am here to carry Your holy Presence, and I am here to carry out Your loving orders. Bless the Lord, O my soul, and all that is within me—all that is within me—bless His holy, wonderful name. Amen and Amen!

Part III

Patterns for a Prayer Storm

Revive Us Again

We praise Thee, O God!
For the Son of Thy love,
For Jesus Who died,
And is now gone above.

(Refrain) *Hallelujah! Thine the glory.*
Hallelujah! Amen.
Hallelujah! Thine the glory.
Revive us again.

We praise Thee, O God!
For Thy Spirit of light,
Who hath shown us our Savior,
And scattered our night.

All glory and praise
To the Lamb that was slain,
Who hath borne all our sins,
And hath cleansed every stain.

All glory and praise
To the God of all grace,
Who hast brought us, and sought us,
And guided our ways.

Revive us again;
Fill each heart with Thy love;
May each soul be rekindled
With fire from above.[1]

Chapter 8

PRAYER FOR REVIVAL IN THE CHURCH

I will heal their backsliding, I will love them freely: for mine anger is turned away from him. I will be as the dew unto Israel: he shall grow as the lily, and cast forth his roots as Lebanon. His branches shall spread, and his beauty shall be as the olive tree, and his smell as Lebanon. They that dwell under his shadow shall return; they shall revive as the corn, and grow as the vine: the scent thereof shall be as the wine of Lebanon (Hosea 14:4-7 KJV).

John Wesley was once asked how he managed to gather such large crowds to listen to him preach. His response was immediate: "I set myself on fire, and people come to watch me burn!"[2] Where does that kind of fire come from? That kind of revival fire is ignited by the burning lampstand of fervent intercession.

What does a fire do? It warms and enlightens. It purifies. It empowers. A spiritual fire does the same things as a natural fire—it warms up a cold heart and makes it desire God. It releases the revelation like rays of light so that, suddenly, it's as if "the lights just came on." It burns sin out and brings cleansing to hearts and souls. And it releases new zeal and power into a believer's life. When we're praying for revival, we're praying for revival fire. We're praying for a firestorm.

WHAT IS REVIVAL?

Only something that was once alive can be revived. In other words, revival isn't the same as birth. You can revive a drowned person, but what you're doing is bringing that person back to the life that he or she already had before they drowned. Revival means the return to life or the recovery from death or apparent death.

Revival also means a return to activity after a season of lethargy, apathy, and languor. It's like a shock to the system. Emotions rise again as spirits are revived. Isaiah portrays this aspect of revival:

Oh, that You would rend the heavens and come down, that the mountains might quake at Your presence—as fire kindles the brushwood, as fire causes water to boil—to make Your name known to Your adversaries, that the nations may tremble at Your presence! When You did awesome things which we did not expect, You came down, the mountains quaked at Your presence (Isaiah 64:1-3).

Revival also applies to the recovery of a vital truth from oblivion, neglect, or obscurity, or, in other words, to the return to life of something that has been forgotten. This is easy to see in spiritual terms, because in times of spiritual revival, long-neglected truths are restored to life, and people rejoice to learn and obey them once again. In a time of revival, people renew their interest in spiritual concerns, their hearts and souls are restored with fresh life, and they are eager to engender more life wherever they go. Spiritual revival is so powerful that society itself can be transformed.

Colin Dye, whose church, Kensington Temple, in London, England, is one of the largest churches in Europe, is a scholar and a statesman as well as a pastor. Here is what he says about revival:

> Revival is a season of a powerful visitation from God. The term, properly speaking, belongs to the history of the Church subsequent to the New Testament era. However, during the historic revivals we can identify dominant elements that are also present in the New Testament Church. These center on God acting through powerful manifestations of His presence, strengthening the Church, and awakening the world. Indeed, there are many features of revival that flow out of the New Testament experience of God: conviction of sin, many conversions, powerful spiritual encounters, revelations of God, great assurance of salvation, spiritual fervor, and some kind of lasting legacy for the Church and society at large.[3]

You see here that revival involves a visitation from God in which His presence is powerfully and tangibly manifested in order to strengthen the Church and awaken the sleeping world to His reality. People in the midst of revival are convicted of sin, converted to faith, impressed with God's truth, and propelled into firsthand experiences of a spiritual nature—and this has lasting results.

In the Bible, we can find prayers for revival. I have already quoted Isaiah's impassioned plea for God to "rend the heavens and come down." The sons of Korah, who were psalmists, and the prophet Habakkuk also prayed for God's life to be rekindled in the lives of His people:

> *You showed favor to Your land, O Lord; You restored the fortunes of Jacob. You forgave the iniquity of Your people and covered all their sins. Selah. You set aside all Your*

wrath and turned from Your fierce anger. Restore us again, O God our Savior, and put away Your displeasure toward us. Will You be angry with us forever? Will You prolong Your anger through all generations? Will You not revive us again, that Your people may rejoice in You? (Psalm 85:1-6 NIV).

Lord, I have heard of Your fame; I stand in awe of Your deeds, O Lord. Renew them in our day, in our time make them known; in wrath remember mercy (Habakkuk 3:2 NIV).

These Scriptures are like "prayer ammo." We can use them over and over.

Before the revival in the Hebrides islands off Scotland, in 1949, two elderly sisters and several young men prayed those words from Isaiah 64:1 over and over for weeks and months: "Lord, rend the heavens and come down!" They also prayed from the words of Isaiah 44:3-4:

For I will pour water upon him that is thirsty, and floods upon the dry ground: I will pour My spirit upon thy seed, and My blessing upon thine offspring: And they shall spring up as among the grass, as willows by the water courses (Isaiah 44:3-4 KJV).

Their fervent pleas were rewarded when God's Spirit fell on the islands to such a degree that spontaneous conversions occurred everywhere and the crime rate plummeted. It became one of the most phenomenal outpourings of the Holy Spirit since the Day of Pentecost.

The sisters, Christine and Peggy Smith, 82 and 84 years old, were too frail to leave their cottage, located in the village of Barvas on the island of Lewis, to attend worship services. Peggy was blind, and Christine was crippled with arthritis. So they prayed from home. They prayed twice a week. They would get on their knees at ten o'clock in the evening, and they never stopped praying until three or four o'clock in the morning.

After God gave them a vision of revival in their parish church, a group of young men who were office-holders in the parish began to pray as well, and they prayed together twice a week in a cold barn, on Tuesday and Friday nights. Sometimes the men were forced to crawl inside of the haystacks in order to keep warm. Under the inspiration of the Holy Spirit, these nine ordinary Scots prayed without a letup for a month and a half, pleading with God to send revival to their community and beyond.

One night, a deacon stood up and read from Psalm 24:

Who shall ascend into the hill of the Lord? Or who shall stand in His holy place? He that hath clean hands, and a pure heart; who hath not lifted up his soul unto vanity, nor sworn deceitfully. He shall receive the blessing [notice that it's "the" blessing, not "a" blessing] *from the Lord, and righteousness from the God of his salvation. This is the generation of them that seek Him, that seek Thy face, O Jacob* (Psalm 24:3-6 KJV).

Before he sat down, he challenged his fellow intercessors—and himself—by asking God, "God, are my hands clean? Is my heart pure?" He could not go any further, because he fell on the floor of the barn under the power of the Spirit. All of those present were convicted of how essential holiness was to those who would expect a visitation from God.

Soon after, the elderly sisters urged their pastor to bring in an evangelist, because in a vision, one of them had seen a man who was not from their village speaking in the pulpit. After a series of inquiries, he brought a young man named Duncan Campbell to speak. Here is a small portion of Campbell's own account of what happened on the very first night, told almost 20 years later. Here is what happened just after he had finished preaching to a congregation of about three hundred people.

Just as I am walking down the aisle, along with this young deacon who read the Psalm in the barn. He suddenly stood in the aisle and looking up to the heavens he said, "God, You can't fail us. God, You can't fail us. You promised to pour water on the thirsty and floods upon the dry ground—God, You can't fail us!"

Soon he is on his knees in the aisle, and he is still praying, and then he falls into a trance again. Just then the door opened—it is now eleven o'clock. The door of the church opens, and the local blacksmith comes back into the church and says, "Mr. Campbell, something wonderful has happened. Oh, we were praying that God would pour water on the thirsty and floods upon the dry ground and listen, He's done it! He's done it!"

When I went to the door of the church I saw a congregation of approximately 600 people. Six hundred people—where had they come from? What had happened? I believe that that very night God swept in Pentecostal power—the power of the Holy Ghost. And what happened in the early days of the apostles was happening now in the parish of Barvas.

Over 100 young people were at the dance in the parish hall and they weren't thinking of God or eternity. God was not in all of their thoughts. They were there to have a good night when suddenly the power of God fell upon the dance. The music ceased, and in a matter of minutes, the hall was empty. They fled from the hall as a man fleeing from a plague. And they made for the church. They are now standing outside. Oh, yes—they saw lights in the church. That was a house of God and they were going to it and they went. Men and women who had gone to bed rose, dressed, and made for the church. Nothing in the way of publicity—no mention of a special effort except an intonation from the pulpit on Sabbath that a certain man was going to be conducting a series of meetings in the parish covering 10 days. But God took the situation in hand—oh, He became His own publicity agent. A hunger and a thirst gripped the people. 600 of them now are at the church standing outside.[4]

Duncan Campbell far exceeded the ten-day time period he had agreed to stay. The first wave of the revival lasted five weeks. Prayer meetings were held day and night throughout the parishes. Then there was a brief lull, followed by weeks more. The revival was not accompanied by healings or by speaking in tongues, but everyone experienced remarkable, repeated, power-encounters with God. Bold prayers were prayed—and answered. Incorrigible sinners were saved, many of whom went on to lead many others to Christ. An astonishing number of those who were saved were young people, very few of whom ever stopped following Jesus for the rest of their lives, and many of whom are still alive today, of course, because all of this happened only in the middle of the 20th century.[5]

The reason I tell you this story is because it helps answer the question, "What is revival?" Although the specifics may differ from place to place and from time to time, some of them will always be present in a true revival, not the least of which is always fervent, concentrated, persistent intercessory prayer.

THE ROLE OF PRAYER IN SPIRITUAL AWAKENING

Without prayer, revival will not come. But what does this kind of prayer look like? In 1976, an Oxford-educated church historian named J. Edwin Orr gave a talk entitled "The Role of Prayer in Spiritual Awakening" at the National Prayer Congress in Dallas. A videotape of his presentation was made, and it is still available today. Here are some excerpts from it:

> Dr. A.T. Pierson once said, "There has never been a spiritual awakening in any country or locality that did not begin in united prayer." Let me recount what God has done through concerted, united, sustained prayer.

> Not many people realize that in the wake of the American Revolution there was a moral slump.... [Crime, drunkenness, profanity rose to alarming levels. Churches stopped growing and began to shrink.] Christians were so few on [the campuses of Ivy League colleges] in the 1790s that they met in secret, like a communist cell, and kept their minutes in code so that no one would know....The Chief of Justice of the United States, John Marshall, wrote to the Bishop of Virginia, James Madison, that the Church "was too far gone ever to be redeemed." Voltaire averred, and Tom Paine echoed, "Christianity will be forgotten in thirty years."

> ...How did the situation change? It came through a concert of prayer....In New England, there was a man of prayer named Isaac Backus, a Baptist pastor who in 1794, when conditions were at their worst, addressed

an urgent plea for prayer for revival to pastors of every Christian denomination in the United States.

Churches knew that their backs were to the wall, so the Presbyterians of New York, New Jersey, and Pennsylvania adopted it for all their churches. Bishop Francis Asbury adopted it for all the Methodists. The Congregational and Baptist Associations, the Reformed and the Moravians all adopted the plan, until America...was interlaced with a network of prayer meetings, which set aside the first Monday of each month to pray.

It was not too long before the revival came. It broke out first of all in Connecticut, then spread to Massachusetts and all the seaboard states, in every case entirely without extravagance or outcry. [In the summer of 1800, when it reached Kentucky, which was a lawless territory at the time, it burst into wildfire. Great camp meetings were held, and pastors of every denominational affiliation assisted when as many as 11,000 people came to one communion service.]

Out of that second great awakening...came the whole modern missionary movement and its societies. Out of it came the abolition of slavery, popular education, Bible societies, Sunday schools and many social benefits....

[However, by the mid-1800s, conditions had deteriorated again.] In September 1857, a man of prayer, Jeremiah Lanphier, started a prayer meeting in the upper room of the Dutch Reformed Church consistory building in Manhattan. In response to his advertisement, only six people out of the population of a million showed up. But, the following week, there were fourteen, and then twenty-three, when it was decided to meet every day for prayer. By late winter, they were filling the Dutch Reformed Church, then the Methodist Church on John Street, then Trinity Episcopal Church on Broadway at Wall Street. In February and March of 1858, every church and public hall in downtown New York was filled. Horace Greeley, the famous editor, sent a reporter with horse and buggy racing around the prayer meetings to see how many men were praying: in one hour, he could get to only twelve meetings, but he counted 6100 men attending. Then a landslide of prayer began, which overflowed to the churches in the evenings. People began to be converted, ten thousand a week in New York City alone. The movement spread throughout New England, the church bells bringing people to prayer at eight in the morning, twelve noon, six in the evening. The revival raced up the Hudson and down the Mohawk, where the Baptists, for example, had so many people to baptize that they went down to the river, cut a big hole in the ice, and baptized them in the cold water: when Baptists do that they really are on fire….[Out of this revival came a young shoe salesman whose name became a household word, D.L. Moody.]…More than a million people were converted to God in one year out of a population of thirty million.

Then that same revival jumped the Atlantic appeared in Ulster, Scotland, Wales, then England, parts of Europe, South Africa and South India, anywhere there was an evangelical cause. It sent mission pioneers to many countries. Effects were felt for forty years. Having begun in a movement of prayer, it was sustained by a movement of prayer.

That movement lasted for a generation, but at the turn of the twentieth century, there was need of awakening again. A general movement of prayer began, with special prayer meetings at Moody Bible Institute; at Kenswick Convention in England; and places as far apart as Melbourne, Australia; Wonsan in Korea; and Nilgiri Hills of India. So all around the world believers were praying that there might be another great awakening in the twentieth century....

[Among the most notable results of this prayer is the well-known Welsh Revival of 1904] ...The movement went like a tidal wave over Wales. In five months there were a hundred thousand people converted throughout the country....It was the social impact that was astounding. For example, judges were presented with white gloves, not a case to try: no robberies, no burglaries, no rapes, no murders and no embezzlements, nothing....As the revival swept Wales, drunkenness was cut in half. There was a wave of bankruptcies, but they were nearly all for taverns. There was even a slowdown in the mines. You say, "How could a religious revival cause a strike?" It did not cause a strike, just a slowdown, for so many Welsh coal miners were converted and stopped using bad language that the horses that dragged the trucks in the mines could not understand what was being said to them, hence transportation slowed down for a while until they learned the language of Canaan. (When I first heard that story, I thought that it was a tall tale, but I can document it.) That revival also affected sexual moral standards, I had discovered through the figures given by British government experts that, in Radnorshire and Merionethshire, the actual illegitimate birth rate had dropped 44% within a year of the beginning of the revival. That revival swept Britain. It so moved all of Norway that the Norwegian Parliament passed special legislation to permit laymen to conduct Communion because the clergy could not keep up with the number of the converts desiring to partake. It swept Sweden, Finland and Denmark, Germany, Canada from coast to coast, all of the United States, Australia, New Zealand, South Africa, East Africa, Central Africa, West Africa, touching also Brazil, Mexico, and Chile....

As always, it began through a movement of prayer, with prayer meetings all over the United States as well as the other countries; and soon there came the great time of the harvest. So what is the lesson we can learn? It is a very simple one, as direct as the promises of God in Scripture: "If My people, who are called by My name, shall humble themselves and pray, and seek My face, and turn from their wicked ways, then I will hear from heaven and will forgive their sin and will heal their land" (2 Chron. 7:14 RSV).

What is involved in this? As God requires us to pray, we must not forget what was said by Jonathan Edwards: "...to promote explicit agreement and visible union of God's people in extraordinary prayer." What do we mean by extraordinary prayer? We share in ordinary prayer in regular worship services, before eating and the like. But when people are found getting up at six in the morning to pray, or having a half night of prayer until midnight, or giving up their lunchtime to pray at a noonday prayer meeting, that is extraordinary prayer. But it must be united and concerted.[6]

Dr. Orr touched on just a few highlights from the 19th and 20th centuries. Again and again, we see the powerful effect of prayer in bringing about true revival. It takes a lot of prayer to bring true revival. It takes an army of intercessors praying over time. Those who pray for revival do not need to be in the same room at the same time, although sometimes they are. They don't even need to speak the same language, because they might come from different countries. But they do need to be united in purpose: "Lord, send Your Spirit. Revive us again! Rend the heavens and come down!"

REVIVAL PRELIMINARIES

Prayer is an absolute prerequisite for revival. It stems from a hunger and an intense desire for *change*. Something simply must change in the situation, because the situation is intolerable. Or—tell me if you have not experienced this yourself—it's more as if something must change in the situation, because the situation is just plain boring! You know what I mean. You have gone along for some time, and nothing has seemed very exciting. Church just isn't quite meeting your needs. You can't figure out what your purpose is, and you're not sure the people around you know what theirs is either. You can't quite put your finger on what's wrong, but you get frustrated with it. In times like these, your heart and mouth can release grumbling and accusation—or prayer. If you want to get out of the doldrums and into revival, choose prayer. Prayer definitely changes things.

Another prerequisite for revival is networking. People begin to pull together in *unity*. They begin to pool their efforts and their prayers. They begin to cry out with one voice: "Lord, we need You! We are hungry for You. We are utterly dependent upon You." The relational work of networking results in progress toward unified prayer with an identifiable goal. Praying as a team gives feet to your restlessness and hope in the midst of your spiritual hunger.

In the Nashville area where I live, different congregations and ministries host a Call2Worship periodically on Sunday nights. It's just a small piece of the big picture, but it's an important one. It builds citywide unity, promotes hunger for the Lord, and releases the power of corporate worship and prayer. Those prayers hit their targets! They don't just bounce off the ceiling. What makes the difference is that we pray together; we have united across denominational and cultural lines to seek God's face for the sake of our city and region.

WHAT REVIVAL LOOKS LIKE

Prayer is a key ingredient prior to revival, and prayer continues as a key ingredient for sustaining the results of revival. What are we looking for when we pray for revival? And what does it look like to sustain revival when the Holy Spirit brings it?

There are five primary characteristics of true, classic revival: (1) an experiential conviction of sin, which results in (2) a passionate denunciation of sin because of (3) a revelation of God's holiness, (4) a deep awareness of God's love and mercy, and (5) a sometimes painfully heightened consciousness of eternity. These characteristics can be illustrated abundantly from the Scriptures and from the history of the ebb and flow of the Christian faith.

For example, David Brainerd, who went out into the forests and preached to the natives in early America, prayed for days at a time, outdoors. He longed to portray the Lord Jesus Christ as a kind and compassionate master, and he would intercede and plead with his listeners to accept the mercy of God—and they did. Even though Brainerd's life was cut short, most likely because of the hardships he endured, the results of his prayer and preaching brought the Kingdom to a people group who had lived in spiritual darkness for generations.

A classic example from the same time period is Jonathan Edwards, whose prayers and sermons helped to usher in the First Great Awakening in colonial America. His preaching was not "seeker friendly," but seekers—often with much emotion—did find salvation at the feet of the living God. Edwards' most famous sermon is titled, "Sinners in the Hands of an Angry God," and others bear such appealing titles as "Wrath Upon the Wicked for the Uttermost," "Eternity of Hell's Torments," and "Justice of God in the Damnation of Sinners." Edwards' passion was not so much that sin would be exposed and punished as it was that God's overwhelming mercy would be given an opportunity to reach people's hearts. The heart-revival that he spearheaded swept across the colonies and effected broad societal changes, influencing the future spiritual climate of an entire continent.

PRAYER BEFORE REVIVAL, DURING REVIVAL, AND AFTER REVIVAL

Prayer, and more prayer, is the appropriate response to desperate times. Extreme prayer at all hours of the day and night is the only appropriate application of effort before, during, and after a time of revival from God. God wants to revive His people, wherever they may live. In other words, revival is *His* work, and the way we participate is to engage *Him* in all prayerfulness.

Charles Finney, who was known for his phenomenal evangelistic successes during the Second Great Awakening in the United States, had equally phenomenal prayer support behind the scenes. He is quoted as having said, "Revival is no more a miracle than a crop of wheat. Revival comes from heaven when heroic souls enter the conflict determined to win or die—or if need be, to win and die."[7]

Matthew Henry, an English theologian and clergyman who predates Finney, Edwards, and Brainerd and who composed the massive commentaries to the Old and New Testaments that bear his name, wrote, "When God intends to do great mercy for his people, the first thing he does is to set them a-praying."[8]

Not just any kind of prayer will do. This kind of praying makes you sweat. It is hard work. It's often compared to the travail of childbirth. Leonard Ravenhill, a 20th-century British revivalist, once said, "At God's counter there are no sale days, for the price for revival is ever the same—travail."[9]

E.M. Bounds, a Civil-War-era preacher and author who wrote prolifically about the importance of prayer, especially as it applies to all forms and stages of revival, wrote,

> The wrestling quality of importunate prayer does not spring from physical vehemence or fleshly energy. It is not an impulse of energy, nor mere earnestness of soul. It is an inwrought force, a faculty implanted and aroused by the Holy Spirit. Virtually, it is the intercession of the Holy Spirit in us.[10]

Bounds had laid hold of the same truth that Jesus expressed to His disciples: "...The kingdom of heaven suffers violence and the violent take it by force" (Matt. 11:12 NKJV).

Prayer for revival, which is one of the four primary emphases of Prayer Storm, is prayer for the Kingdom of God to come *here* and *now*. The only effective prayer is that which is inspired by the Holy Spirit, and that prayer, by definition, is going to be "violent," passionate, and untiringly persistent.

This kind of prayer will incur opposition. Persecution, opposition, and challenge are guaranteed. No advance of the Kingdom goes unchallenged; what you challenge will challenge you back. If you target individuals in prayer, persecution will come to you from individuals. If you target the Church in prayer, opposition will come from the Church. If you target the society around you, some segment of that society will fight back.

Therefore, you need even more fervency and even more of the Spirit of revival. Like those who have gone before you, you need to press forward, undaunted, linked arm-in-arm and spirit-to-spirit with your fellow intercessors, walking together through the conflict with other prayer warriors until victory is achieved. And then, after revival has come, you must support each other in the great work of stewarding the longed-for move of God.

> *In the name of Jesus, we labor with His Holy Spirit for a God-sent revival in our day. We will not quit praying until we have seen with our own eyes the glory of the Lord covering the earth as the waters cover the seas. O God, release a global revival to the Church in our day! Awaken the sleeping beauty called the Body of Christ to her destiny. Start in our nation! Start in my city! Start in my congregation! Start in my family! Start in my very own heart! Release revival fire for the sake of Your holy name! Amen and Amen.*

Mighty Army of the Young

Mighty army of the young,
Lift your voice in cheerful song,
Send the welcome word along—Jesus lives!
Once He died for you and me,
Bore our sins upon the tree,
Now He lives to make us free—Jesus lives!

(Refrain) *Wait not till the shadows lengthen, till you older grow,*
Rally now and sing for Jesus, ev'rywhere you go;
Lift your joyful voices high,
Ringing clear thro' earth and sky,
Let the blessèd tidings fly—Jesus lives!

Voice of youth so glad and free,
Sing your song of victory;
Sing to all on land and sea—Jesus lives!
Light for you and all mankind,
Sight of all by sin made blind,
Life in Jesus all may find—Jesus lives!

Jesus lives, O blessèd words!
King of kings, and Lord of lords!
Lift the cross and sheathe the swords—Jesus lives!
See, He breaks the prison wall,
Throws aside the dreadful pall,
Conquers death at once for all—Jesus lives![1]

Chapter 9

Prayer for Another Great Awakening—Youth

And it shall come to pass afterward that I will pour out My Spirit on all flesh; your sons and your daughters shall prophesy, your old men shall dream dreams, your young men shall see visions. And also on My menservants and on My maidservants I will pour out My Spirit in those days (Joel 2:28-29 NKJV).

The time has come for another Great Awakening! More than 40 years ago, in 1967, a youth revival started that was called the Jesus People movement, and it swept across the country, exploding in colleges and coffeehouses. People were being saved everywhere. It was radical.

It was also during that year that the Catholic charismatic renewal, one of the largest movements in neo-pentecostal history, got its start. A group of professors at Duquesne University in Pittsburgh, Pennsylvania, sparked a fire among their students after they themselves were baptized in the Holy Spirit, and the fire quickly spread to the University of Notre Dame in Indiana and then to the University of Michigan and around the world. Though this charismatic move had its beginning among young people in a Catholic university, it was not limited to that setting. Thousands upon thousands of people of all ages from mainline Protestant denominations were ushered into fresh encounters with Jesus and the baptism in the Holy Spirit. Prayer gatherings were started. Healings occurred. Celebrations of praise became the hallmark of the movement as the Spirit of Jesus was welcomed back into His rightful place.

Now, more than 40 years later, we are crying out, "Do it again, God! Way beyond the Jesus People movement! Way beyond the charismatic movement! Do it again, God! Do it again in this generation! We're heading around a corner. It happened before. It can happen again. It's time for another great awakening of youth. Why not have the greatest youth awakening that the world has ever seen?

REVOLUTION—ALWAYS BEGINS WITH YOUNG ADULTS

Almost every revolution you have ever heard of started with students on a college or university campus. Throughout history, it seems to be the case that revolutions get started, both bad ones and good ones, because student-aged young people are hungry for change and willing to lay down their lives for a cause, whether it's political, social, or spiritual. Think of revolutions such as Marxism, Nazism, and Communism, or Pentecostalism and the Jesus People movement.

Campuses, of course, are where the future leaders are collected together in one place and are being trained. They are influenced by powerful voices and trends, and they influence each other. Educational institutions also host many young people from other countries. In fact, there are more than 550,000 international students attending American universities currently. Young adulthood is a time of great change. For example, statistics show that more than 77 percent of all Christians made their decisions for Christ before they turned 21 years of age.[2]

A spiritual awakening among young adults is, therefore, a prophetic promise for an entire generation. If Christians can reach campuses for Christ, God can in turn reach cities and nations. The words that the apostle Paul wrote to the young man Timothy can apply to young adults on campuses today:

> *I'm passing this work on to you, my son Timothy. The prophetic word that was directed to you prepared us for this. All those prayers are coming together now so you will do this well, fearless in your struggle, keeping a firm grip on your faith and on yourself. After all, this is a fight we're in* (1 Timothy 1:18-19 TM).

Throughout Christian history, spiritual battles result in spiritual awakenings, and young people are clearly at the center.

CAMPUS MINISTRY, CAMBRIDGE STYLE

In 1799, an evangelical move of the Holy Spirit began at King's College, Cambridge, England. It began with the conversion of a student named Charles Simeon. This movement progressed slowly but surely for years, until there was enough evangelical activity that, by 1877, students from across Cambridge's 17 colleges organized the Cambridge Inter-Collegiate Christian Union (CICCU), which in turn caused an increased interest in salvations and missions. An evangelistic campaign led by D.L. Moody and Ira Sankey resulted in a noticeable increase in enrollment in theology schools and involvement in missions, including the launching of the "Cambridge Seven" to China, led by C.T. Studd, who had been a well-known cricket player.[3] More than a century later, CICCU still exists as Cambridge's longest-tenured student group, and CICCU has helped with the formation of InterVarsity organizations across Great Britain and North America. Campus ministries such as InterVarsity, Campus Crusade for Christ, and the Navigators have helped immeasurably to spur the growth of evangelical faith over the past 50-plus years.[4]

EVAN ROBERTS AND THE WELSH REVIVAL OF 1904

Young Evan Roberts began to seek the Lord when he was only 13 years old. By the time he was 26, his earnest, prayerful efforts brought revival to his hometown in Wales. In a short time, the Spirit of God came so powerfully that 100,000 people across the country gave their lives to Christ, and the effects of that Welsh Revival are still being felt today, especially because of its contributions to the birth of pentecostalism in the United States and across the world. Evan Roberts' simple prayer was "Send the Spirit now for Jesus Christ's sake," and "Send the Spirit now more powerfully for Jesus Christ's sake." He was a young man, but people of all ages responded to the Gospel message because of his revolutionary zeal and his humble, prayerful, obedience to the Holy Spirit.

THE ROLE OF PRAYER IN STUDENT REVIVALS

In order to understand revival, we must understand the role of prayer in the history of revivals. J. Edwin Orr, the famous revival historian, said, "Young people in student-led prayer cells have been at the forefront in almost every awakening."[5] For example, the Moravian 24/7 prayer and missionary movement that was started in 1727 by Count Nicolas Ludwig von Zinzendorf was built on his youthful zeal. By the time he graduated from the equivalent of high school at the age of 16, Zinzendorf had started no fewer than seven different student prayer groups, and he continued his prayer disciplines while he was a student at the University of Wittenberg from 1716 to 1719.

The First Great Awakening in North America and Europe was ignited by a Yale University graduate named Jonathan Edwards and by Oxford students John Wesley and George Whitefield. The Second Great Awakening was sparked by

Timothy Dwight, the grandson of Jonathan Edwards, at Yale University. After his 1797 message to Yale students, nearly half of Yale's student body came to Christ in a few short months.

Samuel Mills was a freshman at Williams College, in Massachusetts, in 1806, when he met with four friends for prayer about revival and world missions. When a rainstorm hit, they took refuge under a haystack and continued to pray (thus becoming known as the "Haystack Five").

> When the rain subsided, Mills stood up, slammed his fist into his hand, and announced, "We can do this, if we will!" These five young collegians stepped out in faith and not only initiated the first nationwide student movement, but also began the first six mission agencies from North America. Although there were just 25 colleges in America (averaging about a hundred students each) at the time, the "Haystack Five" helped launch small world mission study and prayer clusters on many of them.[6]

About 80 years later, a 20-something young man named Luther Wishard, who had just been appointed as a leader in the YMCA, heard the story of the Haystack Five. Inspired by the story, he committed himself to a revival of the same vision, and went on to found the Student Volunteer Movement, which became the largest missions movement of all time.

> Over the next generation, students on every campus in the U.S. committed themselves to the "evangelization of the world in this generation." Over 20,000 of them sailed to the foreign mission field, and over 80,000 others had personally committed themselves to prayer and to financially support those being sent out.[7]

These are just a few examples of the phenomenal revival zeal that comes out of the college-age generation.

PROPHETIC PROMISES OF A GREAT YOUTH MOVEMENT

If you read your Bible with an eye toward young adults, you can see how readily God engages that generation for His purposes—even before colleges and universities existed. Biblical prophecies about the first and second comings of Christ are not confined to the prophetic books of the Old Testament. A surprising number are found in the Psalms. Here's an example:

> *The Lord says to my Lord: "Sit at My right hand until I make Your enemies a footstool for Your feet." The Lord will extend Your mighty scepter from Zion; You will rule in the midst of Your enemies. Your troops will be willing on Your day of battle. Arrayed in holy majesty, from the womb of the dawn You will receive the dew of Your youth* [or Your young men will come to You like the dew] (Psalm 110:1-3 NIV).

This psalm portrays God the Father speaking to His Son Jesus, while David observes and narrates by writing the words of the psalm. David describes Jesus being revealed as the Messiah, whose "mighty scepter" will be extended from Zion. Where is Zion? It is not as much a physical place as it is a presence, specifically the presence of God giving glory to His people in the messianic age. Wherever God's authority has been established, He lives and works. Zion can be among the believing Jews of the old covenant as well as the believers of the new covenant of the Body of Christ.

The Father's mighty scepter of power will be stretched forth from "Zion," because His authority has been transferred to His people, and they will be able to rule with Him, even in the midst of their enemies. They will volunteer freely, abandoning their former plans in order to walk in holiness and obedience, carrying out God's will and accomplishing His purpose. This won't apply to just one or two people but rather to a host of them, largely young people, who will appear like the dew on the ground.

I for one want to be one of those "young" people. I want to see young men and women coming to the Lord, and I want my youth to be renewed in the process. Most of all, I want to be one of those who is privileged to usher in the Kingdom of God in the age in which we live. I want to encourage young people as they respond to God's invitation to serve Him.

In 1995, I had an intense dream and visionary experience in which I saw stadiums filled with young people praising God. I heard this piercing word, "Out of the belly of the Promise Keepers Movement shall come forth a Youth Extravaganza that will rock the nations. The stadiums will be filled as out of the belly of the Promise Keepers movement shall come forth a Youth Extravaganza that will rock the nations." I'm expecting to see the fulfillment of this word.

Notice He didn't say "stadium," singular, nor did He say "nation," singular. *Stadiums* and *nations* will be filled and rocked. In my vision, I saw a large football stadium filled with young people and adults who were radically worshipping and praising God, and I saw a laser-beam light show crisscrossing the sky. Then the lights met high in the sky above the stadium and formed into a cross. On a giant Jumbotron at the end of the stadium, I saw a depiction of the passion of Christ, with a close-up of the hammer coming down upon the nail that was being driven through the wrist of Yeshua (Jesus). In the background, I heard the line from the old Jesus People song that was sung by Randy Matthews, "Didn't He"—"And the hammer fell on the wooden nail."[8] As the hammer fell and the cross shone in the sky, a spirit of conviction fell upon the audience, and the people began to cry out and even shriek to the Lord for mercy.

The central focus of the youth awakening will be the cross of Jesus, lifted high for all to see. Giant gatherings will occur across this nation and other nations as the world is swept in an unprecedented move of worship, prayer, and fasting. This is what we are praying and working toward. This is going to happen because of the intense prayer storm that precedes it, the prayer gatherings and the all-night prayer vigils and the solemn assemblies that unite the generations across the nation.

Twenty years before my vision, in 1975, Bob Jones, who has had a great prophetic influence on my life, had the first of a series of encounters with angels who spoke about an outpouring of the Spirit that would be characterized by prophetic intercession; this appeared to Bob like an atomic explosion of light. Then, in January of 1984, the Lord showed Bob that prophetic intercession would need to be joined by "compassion and worship" to be complete. These elements needed to cross-pollinate each other. The combination of these anointings would result in several things: (1) revival in the Church, (2) power evangelism in world missions, (3) justice in society, (4) pockets of mercy ("cities of refuge"), and (5) worldwide intercession for Israel. Between 1975 and 1983, Bob was given over 100 prophetic revelations about a worldwide youth movement that would rise up. (Earlier, Bob had been brought back from a near-death experience so that he could be used to anoint the next generation of leaders who would help usher into the Kingdom one billion souls.) All signs point to a worldwide youth awakening.

We're seeing a number of exciting developments in these days that show us that these prophecies and many others are being fulfilled. The 24/7 prayer movement is one example, as is the explosion of TheCall, the stadium-based prayer and intercession gatherings of young people that Lou Engle has spearheaded. At TheCall Nashville, on 7/7/07, the stadium was completely filled with 75,000 people. This was the first time that one of TheCall worship/prayer events filled a stadium to capacity. I had the honor of being the chairman of that event, and I felt that it was as if the heavenly birth process was advanced that day. A membrane ruptured, and water was released and "labor" intensified. Someday we will see a fulfillment of the prophetic words and visions.

I am dedicating Prayer Storm to this purpose, and I fully expect the greatest youth awakening that the world has ever of seen. It will happen! With one million consecrated prayer warriors joining in on the Prayer Storm, can anything less happen? Beside becoming a part the Prayer Storm weekly prayer thrust, with one target being the greatest youth awakening that the world has ever seen (www.prayerstorm.com), you can also get practical information about networking and how to start a 24/7 campus house of prayer by going to www. campustransformation.com and www.campusamerica.org. You can also go to www.thecall.com to receive information on participating in one of the many regional, national, and international youth-oriented solemn assemblies for prayer, worship, and fasting.

THE LAW OF NIGHT-AND-DAY PRAYER

Anyone who signs up for Prayer Storm already appreciates the value of 24/7, day-and-night, night-and-day prayer. This Scripture is a familiar one: "And will not God bring about justice for His chosen ones, who cry out to Him day and night? Will He keep putting them off? I tell you, He will see that they get justice, and quickly..." (Luke 18:7-8 NIV). This passage portrays night-and-day prayer. But, you may wonder, why are we convinced that this is what's called for and that it is going to be effective? I have assembled the following list of reasons:

- 24/7 worship and prayer is what is done in Heaven. Let it therefore be done on earth!

- 24/7 worship and prayer releases God's justice on the earth.

- 24/7 worship and prayer fuels the Great Commission (see Matt. 28:19).

- 24/7 worship and prayer hinders the plans of the devil.

- 24/7 worship and prayer releases revival breakthrough.

- 24/7 worship and prayer prepares the way for Christ's second coming.[9]

MATURITY AND STRENGTH

If you want to see an unprecedented harvest of souls, you will be one of those who will pray, pray, and pray some more. We will pray and look forward to the day:

> *When our sons shall be as plants grown large in their youth and our daughters as sculptured corner pillars hewn like those of a palace; when our garners are full, affording all manner of store, and our sheep bring forth thousands and ten thousands in our pastures; when our oxen are well loaded; when there is no invasion [of hostile armies] and no going forth [against besiegers—when there is no murder or manslaughter] and no outcry in our streets; happy and blessed are the people who are in such a case; yes, happy (blessed, fortunate, prosperous, to be envied) are the people whose God is the Lord (Psalm 144:12-15 AMP).*

A grown-up plant is one that has reached maturity and is ready for fruitfulness and productivity. Corner pillars are critical structural supports. If you don't have them, the entire building will collapse. Usefulness in the Kingdom of God is not gender-exclusive or age-limited. It is a matter calling and maturity.

Part of bringing in a youth awakening is recognizing that sons and daughters should be treated as mature and capable. They should be equipped and empowered, according to their giftings, to lay hands on the sick, serve as leaders in the Church, preach, teach, lead worship, baptize new believers, serve communion, cast out demons, and do all kinds of ministry and service. In particular, many young people, because of their ability to think outside the box, can be very useful in helping to devise creative strategies for outreach and a number of other issues. For too many years, the Church has been hampered by a tendency to regard younger believers as ministers-in-waiting, as recruits who must be held back until they are older. The maturing process is not always a factor of chronological age. Psalm 144:12 indicates that we should let our sons in their youth be as full-grown plants—in their *youth*, not after they've been through ten years of training and four years of Bible college and spent another six years in the marketplace. If we wait that long to release our sons and daughters to gather the harvest, it will rot in the field. There is a vital place for formal education and specialized training, of course. But a lack of schooling or a fear of failure should never become excuses to deny young believers opportunities to engage in suitable and appropriate ministries, regardless of age. Look at the end of that psalm: the harvest will be plentiful—as a byproduct of the empowering of the harvesters.

We need to move in the spirit of Elijah, saying "God, give me a spiritual son or daughter." Young people in this "fatherless generation" need to be looking for spiritual parents who will dream with them, encourage them, and intercede for them, helping them tap into their God-given passions and destinies. We need to be elders who will bless (by our word and touch) young people with our time, knowledge, wisdom, strength, vision, and every good thing. We need to treat them like full-grown plants and like corner pillars, bestowing on them a high appraisal of their value and helping them to envision their future in the family of God. We need to help them in practical ways by providing necessary resources and releasing authority to them to accomplish their God-given commissions.

It's not only about information, it's about *impartation*. It's not only about dreams and visions, it's about investment and patience. Responsibility fosters maturity, and maturity leads to greater responsibility to create a joining of the generations. As I have often said, a sustained move of God is comprised of three generations, because God is the God of Abraham, Isaac, and Jacob—three generations walking together as one generation. We need the wisdom of the older, the resources of the middle, and the zeal of the younger. We need the synergy of all three. Regardless of which chronological generation you are a part of, there is one thing every one of them must do, and that's pray. You might not be able to do anything else except pray. Pray up a prayer storm. Pray!

I declare that the greatest youth awakening that the world has ever seen is coming upon the stage of time. Now is the time! This is the generation. The joining of the generations is upon us. My people will volunteer freely in the day of Your power. Let another historic awakening begin now for Jesus Christ's sake!

Lord, we call forth in our day and in this generation the greatest youth awakening that the world has ever seen. You have done it before; now do it again, even better and bigger and more powerfully. Release Your Spirit, and send Your angels to usher in one billion more souls for Your Kingdom, for Jesus Christ's sake. Send revival! Send it now! Move quickly, Holy Spirit, and raise up the greatest youth prayer army of all time. We declare that these prayers are in agreement with Your prophetic purposes for this generation, and we praise Your holy name. Amen and Amen!

I Am Praying for You

I have a Savior, He's pleading in glory,
A dear, loving Savior though earth friends be few;
And now He is watching in tenderness o'er me;
And oh, that my Savior were your Savior, too.

(Refrain) *For you I am praying,*
For you I am praying,
For you I am praying,
I'm praying for you.

I have a Father; to me He has given
A hope for eternity, blessèd and true;
And soon He will call me to meet Him in Heaven,
But, oh, that He'd let me bring you with me, too!

I have a robe; 'tis resplendent in whiteness,
Awaiting in glory my wondering view;
Oh, when I receive it all shining in brightness,
Dear friend, could I see you receiving one, too!

Speak of that Savior, that Father in Heaven,
That harp, crown, and robe which are waiting for you—
That peace you possess, and that rest to be given,
Still praying that Jesus may save them with you.[1]

Chapter 10

Praying Your Family
Into the Kingdom

When He had stepped into the boat, the man who had been controlled by the unclean spirits kept begging Him that he might be with Him. But Jesus refused to permit him, but said to him, "Go home to your own [family and relatives and friends] and bring back word to them of how much the Lord has done for you, and [how He has] had sympathy for you and mercy on you" (Mark 5:18-19 AMP).

As we pray Prayer Storm prayers for crisis intervention, for a youth awakening, for Israel, and for revival, we will keep coming back to the subject of family (and friends, who can often be like family to us). On a personal basis, our crisis intercession very often concerns family-and-friend matters, of course. And when it comes to revival—youth revival or any age revival—it really isn't revival unless it touches our homes and families practically. We want to see revival in our families and homes, in our sphere of relationships. We share the Father's heart to reach our family members.

When we get to Heaven, we will see people from every tribe, tongue, and nation. *Every* tribe or clan will be represented. I want to see my family members there, and so do you! The heavenly multitude is pictured by John in the Book of Revelation:

They sung a new song, saying, "Thou art worthy to take the book, and to open the seals thereof: for Thou wast slain, and hast redeemed us to God by Thy blood out of every kindred, and tongue, and people, and nation" (Revelation 5:9 KJV).

After these things I looked, and behold, a great multitude which no one could count, from every nation and all tribes and peoples and tongues, standing before the throne and before the Lamb, clothed in white robes, and palm branches were in their hands (Revelation 7:9).

In order for these people to stand before the throne at all, they had to believe in the Lord Jesus Christ as the One who was slain for their sins, their Savior. Both of these Scriptures tell us that the multitude represents every "kindred," (tribe, clan), every "tongue" (language), every "people" (culture), and every "nation" (country). The smallest social unit represented is the family; every kindred/tribe/clan indicates every extended family group. Within every ethnic group, different languages are spoken. Within every nation are different people. But among each of the people groups are different "tribes."

Now just put your own family tree into that picture. Some of them you are pretty sure are there already before the throne. Others, you can't be so sure of. But the ones who are currently alive on earth are the ones you can pray for. God wants to populate Heaven with people from every family, every clan, and every tribe on the face of the earth. His angels have enough palm branches for everyone! He is the Father of every one of them, after all:

For this reason [seeing the greatness of this plan by which you are built together in Christ], I bow my knees before the Father of our Lord Jesus Christ, for Whom every family in

heaven and on earth is named [that Father from Whom all
fatherhood takes its title and derives its name] (Ephesians
3:14-15 AMP).

Paul was speaking to us today when he wrote, addressing the
Roman church, "Owe no one anything except to love one
another" (Rom. 13:8a NKJV). Once I heard this statement from
David Wilkerson, pastor and founder of Teen Challenge and
Times Square Church, "Every man who is won in the street is
first won in prayer."[2] I believe it. One of the ways that we pay our
Romans 13:8 "love debt" is to commit our lives to praying oth-
ers into the Kingdom of Heaven. Prayers precede conversions.

PRAYER IN THE GOLL AND WILLARD FAMILIES

My wife and I had family members who prayed for us
before we knew how important prayer was. Clearly, their prayers
had the desired effect in our lives! For both of us, our extended
families are characterized by an unusually large number of
Christians. Michal Ann was blessed with godly, conservative,
believing (Holiness) grandparents. Her grandmother, even on
her deathbed, would ask each one of her grandsons—right in
their faces—whether or not they were walking with Jesus. In
prayer and in action, she marked her lineage for the purposes of
God. We thank God for old-fashioned, believing family members who went before us and paved the way, paying the cost of
praying their lineage into the Kingdom of Heaven.

My own mother was a Hannah; she wasn't barren, but she
was a praying woman. She cried out to God after her first son
was stillborn, "Lord, if you will give me another son, I will dedicate him to Christ's service." I was born exactly one year to the
day later. And I have not known a day in my life when I was not
consciously aware of who Jesus is. I believe that it's because of
my mother's prayers of dedication.

I want to encourage every mother and father—God hears your prayers! Your child is marked when you pray. For the rest of his or her lifetime, a child cannot escape the prayers of a parent. They stick to you and follow you wherever you go.

Whether or not you have natural children, you can still pray with the same effect, because you can become a spiritual mother or father. You can become a travailer, someone who births people into the presence of God. You can part the darkness, at least temporarily, that is trying to dominate and manipulate the lives of those who have come to your attention, and you can call into existence windows of opportunity where the light and mercy of the Good News can dispel the darkness. You can pray for someone's salvation, for that person to walk in righteousness, for that person to walk in grace and obedience to the will of God. Your prayers will be effective.

I don't know what will happen with our four children in the future, but for sure I know that they won't be able to be very successful sinners. Not for long, they won't! I have declared that my lineage will follow Jesus. I have declared, along with Joshua, "...As for me and my house, we will serve the Lord" (Josh. 24:15 KJV).

OUR PRIESTLY ROLE

Praying for our families is just part of our priestly role as members of the priesthood of all believers (see 1 Pet. 2:9). We are called to carry the responsibility and the privilege, along with the authority, to bring others into the presence of the Lord. We're like the priest Aaron in the Book of Exodus, who wore over his heart a breastpiece in which four rows of 12 beautiful stones had been set. Each of the stones symbolized one of the 12 tribes of Israel:

You shall make a breastpiece of judgment, the work of a skillful workman; like the work of the ephod you shall make it: of gold, of blue and purple and scarlet material and fine twisted linen you shall make it. It shall be square and folded double, a span in length and a span in width. You shall mount on it four rows of stones; the first row shall be a row of ruby, topaz and emerald; and the second row a turquoise, a sapphire and a diamond; and the third row a jacinth, an agate and an amethyst; and the fourth row a beryl and an onyx and a jasper; they shall be set in gold filigree. The stones shall be according to the names of the sons of Israel: twelve, according to their names; they shall be like the engravings of a seal, each according to his name for the twelve tribes....Aaron shall carry the names of the sons of Israel in the breastpiece of judgment over his heart when he enters the holy place, for a memorial before the Lord continually. You shall put in the breastpiece of judgment the Urim and the Thummim, and they shall be over Aaron's heart when he goes in before the Lord; and Aaron shall carry the judgment of the sons of Israel over his heart before the Lord continually (Exodus 28:15-21,29-30).

The priest wore the breastpiece of judgment when he entered the holy place to represent the interests of the tribes before the Lord. The priest didn't go to represent himself only. He didn't go into the holy place in a devotional capacity, and neither do you when you bring people before God in prayer. He went in a ministry capacity. He was an ambassador for the tribes whose stones he carried on his chest. So are you when you have someone on your heart (or perhaps an entire family), and you carry them with you into the place where you meet with God.

Who are you carrying on your heart? One of your greatest places of authority will always be within your own family, and one of your greatest privileges will be to carry your family members before God. You go before the throne of God as a believer in Jesus, and you do not represent yourself only. You represent your whole family line.

I represent the nation of Germany, because my Goll heritage is German. I represent the English and the Scots because of my mother's Burns heritage. I represent the two states of the United States where I have been a citizen, Missouri and Tennessee. I carry my current city, Franklin, Tennessee, before the Lord. I carry the families of my church and my neighborhood before the throne. And, of course, I carry to God not only my children, but also my spouse and the members of my extended family. They are all like precious stones, and I am expecting them to become living stones. I have a specialized authority for prayer concerning my heritage.

It will be the same for you. You have a different set of names and places but the same privilege and the same awesome, ambassadorial responsibility. "Household salvation" is on God's heart. You shall be saved—you and your household. (See Acts 16:31.) But it's not automatic. You have to cooperate with the Spirit of God, and you have to discover what He wants you to pray and do. Then, when you stand before Him in prayer, you can wear your breastpiece with stones on it. You can represent your brothers and sisters, your parents, your children, your spouse. You can bring the whole clan to the throne room.

Now, I realize that many of you have come from very difficult family situations, and your current home may be full of strife. Or you may be all alone in the world because your family is far away or gone. This does not present an insurmountable obstacle to the exercise of your priestly privilege. You can overcome a hardened heart and an understandable bitterness. You can repent for your own rebellion and judgmental attitudes. By God's grace, you can pray for those who have hurt you. You can also stand in the gap for others who may not be blood relatives but who have no one else to pray for them. It's part of your priestly responsibility and privilege. Your prayers can make the difference!

Practical Ways of Praying Your Family Into God's Family

I don't know about you, but sometimes it's difficult for me to think of exactly how to pray for somebody. I need very practical tips. Here is a good list of practical ways to pray for family members and friends who are not saved yet or who need a particular kind of help at the moment.

Ask God to Soften Their Hearts

You can pray specifically for the condition of someone's heart to change. You can pray for God to remove the stoniness from a heart and to replace it with softness and receptivity. Prophetically, Ezekiel wrote:

And I will give them one heart [a new heart] and I will put a new spirit within them; and I will take the stony [unnaturally hardened] heart out of their flesh, and will give them a heart of flesh [sensitive and responsive to the touch of their God] (Ezekiel 11:19 AMP).

Hearts can become hard for a lot of reasons, but you can stand in God's presence and ask for a change. You can call out the stoniness so that the Word can find soft soil to be planted in. You can pray for the Word to germinate and grow. You can pray for the truth to become rooted in that heart and to go deep.

Ask God to Send a Spirit of Conviction

You can pray for a spirit of conviction to be released into the heart of the person you are praying for, remembering John 16:8, "And He, when He comes, will convict the world concerning sin and righteousness and judgment." You can say, "I call this one before You, and I ask for a spirit of conviction of sin, righteousness, and judgment to be released. Let him know Your loving kindness and Your mercy. Convince her of eternity. Convince him concerning life and death, of the realities of Heaven and hell. Convince her of the need of a savior."

Ask God to Send a Spirit of Revelation

You can ask for this! You can ask God to send a spirit of wisdom and revelation on your loved ones, to open their minds and hearts to understand the situation. It takes revelation to really know that you need to be saved. It takes revelation to know who Jesus is. Some people get only so far. Their hearts are a little bit softened, and they are a little convicted that, yes, they need religion. But they don't know what it consists of. They need revelation in order to take the next step. Some people begin to have their hearts awakened, and then they go out into the world to try to find God. They need revelation to understand that it's Jesus they're looking for.

Pray for them:

> ...that the God of our Lord Jesus Christ, the Father of glory, may give to you a spirit of wisdom and of revelation in the knowledge of Him. I pray that the eyes of your heart may be enlightened, so that you will know what is the hope

of His calling, what are the riches of the glory of His inheritance in the saints, and what is the surpassing greatness of His power toward us who believe (Ephesians 1:17-19).

If Paul prayed this for people he loved, you can too. God may send a spirit of wisdom and revelation through dreams in the night, visions, or angelic visitations. Or it may come like a gentle dawning. Pray for it!

Ask God to Bring His Word to Remembrance

We learn in John 14 that the Holy Spirit is the Helper, and that He will bring God's truth to a person's remembrance: "But the Helper, the Holy Spirit, whom the Father will send in My name, He will teach you all things, and bring to your remembrance all that I said to you" (John 14:26). If we take that Scripture and couple it with another one, we also see that God intends His Word to accomplish what it was sent to do (see Isa. 55:10-11).

Most people have heard some of God's truth, either when they were children or after they grew up. Maybe it was only from a Christmas card with a Bible verse or a couple of minutes of a television preacher, but if it's God's Word, it has work to do, and your prayers can help. As you pray, call forth the memory of that long-ago Sunday school class. Call forth the recollection of that aunt that the person was so fond of. Call forth the remembrance of that grandfather who said grace before meals. Call forth the often-sung lyrics of that Christmas carol or the recollection of the salvation message from the Billy Graham television special that was broadcast two decades ago.

God is looking for co-laborers, and this could be today's assignment for you. A lot of the Word has gone forth without being watered. You can water it. You may not even know what words or messages the person has absorbed over the years, but you can water God's seeds with your prayers, and you can call it forth to germinate. It may result in a sleepless night for the person you are praying for, but it may also result in a breakthrough that could not have happened otherwise.

Pray Prayers of Forgiveness

You can't pray for people if you still need to forgive them for something. Forgiveness is the master key that unlocks the prison door in a heart of stone. I'm talking about your heart here. You can't pray effective prayers if you have bitterness in your heart. Through forgiveness, you can find identification, faith, and love again.

More than that, you can fully participate in Jesus' model prayer, which is not an individualized prayer from me to the Father, but a corporate one: "*Our* Father who is in heaven.... Give *us* this day *our* daily bread....Forgive us *our* debts [sins]..." (see Matt. 6:9-15). You see, you are praying this for your family. You are identifying with them. "Forgive us." You are stepping into the gap as an intercessor.

If you know of some particular sins of certain family members, pray this way for them to be forgiven. If it's perversion, name it. If it's greed, name it. If it's pride, name it. Even if it's false humility, name it as sin and ask for forgiveness. Repent for it by means of identificational repentance. "And lead us not into temptation, but deliver us from evil. Amen."

Pray for Laborers for the Harvest

This is a prayer that the Lord Jesus recommended. He said, "Ask the Lord of the harvest, therefore, to send out workers into His harvest field" (Matt. 9:38 NIV). When I pray this, I ask the Lord of the harvest to *thrust* forth laborers into the field. The phrase *send out* is a little too mild; the implication is really more like the word *deliverance*, a somewhat violent action. And when I pray this way, I name the fields that are white for the harvest. I say "send forth laborers into the field of So-and-So," naming my backslidden ones, my unchurched ones, my lost ones. I don't do it out of self-righteousness or pride, but in compassion and urgency.

When we pray this way, we have no idea how we have just helped the Holy Ghost to land on someone, to empower that person to release a word of kindness, perform an act of healing, speak a word of encouragement, or utter a word of confrontation. We release laborers into the ripe fields when we pray for laborers in the harvest.

Pray for a Revelation of Eternity

In some ways, praying for a revelation of eternity is like praying for the release of a spirit of conviction. It's not quite the same, though. Here you're asking the Lord to give a person an awareness of the realities of both Heaven and hell. Many people live their whole lives as if this life is all there is. They need to have their eyes opened to the startling reality of an eternal Heaven and hell. They also need to recognize that no one is righteous enough to make it to Heaven without Jesus. You can combine this prayer with a prayer for revelation, asking even for dreams of Heaven and hell. You can combine it with a prayer for remembrance of something they once heard about Heaven or hell. People need a revelation of eternity before they will consider Jesus' invitation to join Him in Heaven. Pray for it for them.

Resist the Enemy

You may find that your prayers are bogged down in something invisible. You may look at the people you're praying for and see no progress at all. It could be the enemy, plain and simple, keeping them from responding to God.

You may say, "Well, I don't know what the powers of darkness are that are hindering my family members." And I would say in response, "What are the issues that hindered *you*?" Often it's as simple as that to identify the problem, because many hindrances are often generational. Other times, you can ask God for insight, and He will give it to you. What is keeping your loved ones from the saving power of Jesus' blood? Address it by name, and rebuke it in Jesus' holy and powerful name. Drive out the darkness so that your loved ones have a chance to see and hear the Good News.

Solicit the Prayers of Others

You can enroll others on your personal intercession team. They too can pray for your family. You can help others pray for their families as well. Paul did this all the time. Look at what he wrote to members of his Church family:

> **Pray on my behalf,** *that utterance may be given to me in the opening of my mouth, to make known with boldness the mystery of the gospel, for which I am an ambassador in chains; that in proclaiming it I may speak boldly, as I ought to speak* (Ephesians 6:19-20).

> *...He will yet deliver us,* **you also joining in helping us through your prayers,** *so that thanks may be given by many persons on our behalf for the favor bestowed on us* **through the prayers of many** (2 Corinthians 1:10-11).

If you can get other people praying with you, you will see progress. Now the Gospel message will penetrate a hard heart. Now healing can occur.

You can partner with people who may have met the family member you're praying for. They may have had only an occasional encounter, but it may be enough to give them a heart for your relative. Or you may partner with intercessors who have never laid eyes on your family member but who are perfectly capable of agreeing with you in prayer. They can endorse your prayers and underline them.

Pray for a Revelation of God's Love

This isn't the last point because it's the least important one. It may be the most important one. Ask God to overwhelm your family member(s) with His love. It's the kindness of God that draws us to repentance (see Rom. 2:4). Of course, He will use difficult circumstances to make someone desperate, but don't pray for Him to send difficulties. Don't partner with the devil's work.

Partner with God, who is good all the time, and pray for a revelation of God's love in the midst of whatever happens. Otherwise, times of crisis will be wasted. If the person doesn't grasp the fact that God loves him or her right in the middle of a grave situation, the person may simply walk away, adjust to it, or otherwise not gain any eternal benefit from it. Even after crying out for help from God, a person can go back to being the same. Our job is to love. God's job is to straighten things out.

BIBLE ILLUSTRATIONS OF PRAYERS FOR FRIENDS AND FAMILY

Let's take a few moments to look at passages that show us how Jesus responded to those who approached Him on behalf of family members or friends.

The Paralytic's Friends

Jesus was at home in Capernaum. He was overwhelmingly popular with the people, and He could minister to them freely there. In one well-known incident, the close friends of a paralyzed man removed the roof of a house to make it possible for their friend to get up close to Him. And Jesus, pleased with the faith and the effort of the man's friends, healed him completely:

> *When He had come back to Capernaum several days afterward, it was heard that He was at home. And many were gathered together, so that there was no longer room, not even near the door; and He was speaking the word to them. And they came, bringing to Him a paralytic, carried by four men. Being unable to get to Him because of the crowd, they removed the roof above Him; and when they had dug an opening, they let down the pallet on which the paralytic was lying. And Jesus seeing their faith said to the paralytic, "Son, your sins are forgiven." (Mark 2:1-5).*

Jesus did not feel imposed upon. He was glad to respond to the "prayers" of the paralytic's friends. All He needed was a chance to act, and He took it. In the same way, we have the special privilege (and the faith) to bring people to His attention. Our friends and family members are "paralyzed" in a way. They can't get to Jesus by themselves. They need someone to carry them to Him.

Jesus appreciated the price the four men paid to lower their friend into His healing presence. They had to be diligent and persevering. They had to sacrifice their own interests. They *knew* He could do a miracle, and their faith caused them to put forth great effort. You will find that there is a price to pay in prayer. It takes love to open the roof (or the heavens). It requires labor. It can be painful. It takes time. But it's worth every bit of effort, isn't it?

The Centurion and His Servant

A Roman centurion had a beloved servant who was ill. He took it upon himself to send for the Great Physician. He put himself forward, asking for help for someone else:

A centurion's servant, whom his master valued highly, was sick and about to die. The centurion heard of Jesus and sent some elders of the Jews to him, asking Him to come and heal his servant. When they came to Jesus, they pleaded earnestly with Him, "This man deserves to have You do this, because he loves our nation and has built our synagogue." So Jesus went with them. He was not far from the house when the centurion sent friends to say to Him: "Lord, don't trouble yourself, for I do not deserve to have You come under my roof. That is why I did not even consider myself worthy to come to You. But say the word, and my servant will be healed. For I myself am a man under authority, with soldiers under me. I tell this one, 'Go,' and he goes; and that one, 'Come,' and he comes. I say to my servant, 'Do this,' and he does it." When Jesus heard this, He was amazed at him, and turning to the crowd following Him, He said, "I tell you, I have not found such great faith even in Israel." Then the men who had been sent returned to the house and found the servant well (Luke 7:2-10 NIV).

Jesus responded immediately. He didn't even need to touch the sick man. He was impressed with the centurion's complete faith in Him, and He healed the sick man from a distance.

Jairus and His Daughter

Jairus had to be persistent to get Jesus to come for the sake of his sick daughter. (See Mark. 5:21-24;35-43.) So many other people wanted Jesus' attention that same day! But he pressed in and persisted until Jesus did come. As we know, it seemed to be too late; his daughter had just died. But Jesus—doing as He seemed to do on a regular basis—interfered with the funeral plans. He raised her from the dead and gave her back to her grateful father. It was the father who made it possible. Jesus wasn't even in the neighborhood when Jairus' daughter became sick. Jairus had to go get Him and lead the way back to his house. That's what we do in prayer all the time!

May revival begin in our own families, in our own homes, for the glory of God's great name. We don't just want revival in a general sense; we want it in a personal way. We want it in our homes and in our families.

Other people prayed for us, and now in turn, we want to pray for those who need more of God. We say "yes" to God's invitation to be ambassadors for His Kingdom. We partner in fervent, effectual prayer with others who may not be part of our families, so that, with Paul, we can walk through doors that used to be closed. (See James 5:16; 1 Corinthians 16:9.)

Release your faith and believe the Lord for more of His presence to come in your family. Stand strong as a prophet and priest in your family, and expect great things! Did you pray for someone while you were reading this chapter? Then you can be sure that things are shifting in the heavenlies. Laborers are being sent. Revelation is on the way. Hearts are melting before the love of Jesus. Yes, you can pray your family into God's family!

Lord, I bring my family members to You right now. I bless them in Jesus' great name. I call on You to soften their hearts and to release a spirit of conviction upon them. I pray that You will reveal Your goodness to them and draw them to repentance. Bring to their remembrance all the good words from You that they have heard from their childhoods, even until this moment. Dispatch laborers to cross their paths, people who will move in power and kindness. Also release demonstrations of Your amazing love to them. I want my family members to be part of Your eternal family. It's all for Your sake, and it's all in Jesus' holy and wonderful name. Amen!

Battle Hymn of the Republic

Mine eyes have seen the glory of the coming of the Lord;
He is trampling out the vintage where the grapes of wrath are stored;
He hath loosed the fateful lightning of His terrible swift sword;
His truth is marching on.

(Refrain) *Glory! Glory! Hallelujah! Glory! Glory! Hallelujah!*
Glory! Glory! Hallelujah! His truth is marching on.

I have seen Him in the watch fires of a hundred circling camps
They have builded Him an altar in the evening dews and damps;
I can read His righteous sentence by the dim and flaring lamps;
His day is marching on. (Refrain:...*His day is marching on.*)

He has sounded forth the trumpet that shall never call retreat;
He is sifting out the hearts of men before His judgment seat;
Oh, be swift, my soul, to answer Him! be jubilant, my feet;
Our God is marching on. (Refrain: ...*Our God is marching on.*)

In the beauty of the lilies Christ was born across the sea,
With a glory in His bosom that transfigures you and me:
As He died to make men holy, let us live to make men free;
While God is marching on.

(Refrain: ...*While God is marching on.*)[1]

Chapter 11

PRAYING FOR PEOPLE IN AUTHORITY

I urge that entreaties and prayers, petitions and thanksgiv-
ings, be made on behalf of all men, for kings and all who
are in authority, so that we may lead a tranquil and quiet
life in all godliness and dignity. This is good and acceptable
in the sight of God our Savior, who desires all men to be
saved and to come to the knowledge of the truth (1 Timothy 2:1-4).

Prayers for people who are in positions of authority have
high priority in the heart of God. We see this in Scriptures such
as the one quoted above. You could even say that First Timothy
2:1-4 is an apostolic admonition for prayer. When South
African pastor and prolific author Andrew Murray read this
passage, he wrote in response:

What a faith in the power of prayer! A few feeble and
despised Christians are to influence the mighty
Roman emperors, and help in securing peace and
quietness. Let us believe that prayer is a power that is
taken up by God in His rule of the world. Let us pray
for our country and its rulers, for all the rulers of the
world, for rulers in cities or districts in which we are
interested. When God's people unite in this, they may
count upon their prayers effecting in the unseen
world more than they know. Let faith hold this fast.[2]

Murray laid hold of the fact that earthly authority cannot be exercised within the will of God without the steady application of prayer on the part of the people of God.

Jack W. Hayford, respected founding pastor of The Church on the Way in Van Nuys, California, comments: "You and I can help decide [whether]…blessing or cursing…happens on earth. We will determine whether God's goodness is released toward specific situations or whether the power of sin and Satan is permitted to prevail. Prayer is the determining factor."[3]

Yes, the prayers that Christians pray for those in authority *matter*; they are essential to the advancement of the Kingdom. We cannot afford to leave them up to others. Prayer for leaders must become one of the features of our lives as intercessors.

Many other Scriptures help us understand how to pray for people who are in positions of authority. Let's look at a few of them:

Honor all people. Love the brotherhood. Fear God. Honor the king (1 Peter 2:17 NKJV).

Fear the Lord and the king, my son, and do not join with the rebellious, for those two will send sudden destruction upon them, and who knows what calamities they can bring? (Proverbs 24:21-22 NIV).

When the righteous are in authority, the people rejoice; but when a wicked man rules, the people groan (Proverbs 29:2 NKJV).

Every person is to be in subjection to the governing authorities. For there is no authority except from God, and those which exist are established by God. Therefore whoever resists authority has opposed the ordinance of God; and they who have opposed will receive condemnation upon themselves. For rulers are not a cause of fear for good behavior, but for evil. Do you want to have no fear of authority? Do what is good and you will have praise from the same; for it is a minister of God to you for good. But if you do what is evil, be afraid; for it does not bear the sword for nothing; for it is a minister of God, an avenger who brings wrath on the one who practices evil. Therefore it is necessary to be in subjection, not only because of wrath, but also for conscience' sake. For because of this you also pay taxes, for rulers are servants of God, devoting them-selves to this very thing. Render to all what is due them: tax to whom tax is due; custom to whom custom; fear to whom fear; honor to whom honor (Romans 13:1-7).

Why should we pray for those who are in authority? I see two reasons in First Timothy 2:1-4:

1. So that "we may lead a tranquil and quiet life in all godliness and dignity"

2. So that God can bring those in authority—as well as those under their authority—to Himself (He "desires all men to be saved and to come to the knowledge of the truth.")

I once heard the late international Bible teacher, Derek Prince, expand on this. He said that it doesn't matter what plans, systems, or programs you devise. If you bypass prayer, you will not have power to carry them out. He compared prayer-less intentions to a building that is wired for electricity— if it's not connected to a power source, nothing will work, even if the wires are in good order and the light fixtures are beauti-ful. Our power-source is prayer, and we are enjoined in the Bible to pray in particular for "kings and all in authority," for good government and wise leadership. Why?

1. So that we might have peace and order

2. For the propagation of the Gospel

3. Because God desires all men to be saved

Another reason that we should pray for those who are in authority is simply to be obedient to the will of God. It's clear that He wants us to pray for those in authority. He also wants us to obey *them* as far as it is possible to do so. If you "do good," as Romans 13:1-7 says, you will have no need to be fearful of the authorities.

I had an interesting experience that illustrates this point very well. When my children were younger and we had first moved to Franklin, Tennessee, I had to make a lot of hurry-up trips to the school to pick up our youngest daughter from basketball practices. Once I was running late, and I was speeding. (I'd like to be able to say that I was too new to the area to know the speed limit, but it was posted clearly.) Wouldn't you know, I heard a siren behind me, and I got pulled over. I'm sure I tossed up some quick "mercy" prayers, you know—"God, have mercy!"

I didn't want to become upset, so I decided to be really, really nice to the policeman. He came over and began to lecture me about how this particular stretch of road has more accidents on it than any other and more fatal accidents, etc. I just kept being nice. But it didn't get me off the hook. He wrote me up a ticket, and I had to make one of those early morning, dreadful court appearances. I thought my mercy prayer didn't work. It also crossed my mind that, even though I talked about praying for those in authority, I hadn't exactly obeyed those in authority in this case. I could try to justify it all away—but the truth is the truth!

Later, in the courtroom, the cases were called in alphabetical order, and "Goll" wasn't too far down the list, especially since some people didn't show up. "James Goll" was called, and I stood up and went forward. They grilled me with the usual questions: "James Goll, have you done this, and did you do that?..."

"Yes, sir," I said, standing there like a tense soldier. "Yes, sir." Then I noticed that the judge was looking at me, totally perplexed. He told me to approach the bench, so reluctantly and cautiously, I did. What was going to happen? The microphone was still on.

"What are you guilty of?" he said.

"Well, sir, you know...." I thought I had already acknowledged everything. "...I was going 17 miles over the speed limit, and..."

He looked at me and said, "Well, all this police officer said that you're guilty of is kindness. In fact, the official wrote that you are 'unusually kind.' You're just guilty of kindness! Case dismissed." And laughter roared out across the entire courtroom. The most surprised person in the courtroom was *me*. (For a moment, I thought I was in a renewal meeting!)

So instead of getting judgment, I got mercy, and I didn't have to pay a thing. I didn't even have to go to one of those drivers' schools, and nothing went onto my record, although I kind of wish that it *had* gone onto my record that I was "guilty of kindness."

WHO SHOULD YOU PRAY FOR?

Don't limit your thinking to only governmental leaders when you talk about praying for people who are in authority. Of course, from a United States government perspective, you should pray for the 16 individuals who make most of the key governmental decisions in the United States: our President, the nine justices of the Supreme Court, the two senators from your state, the U.S. congressperson from your district, the governor of your state, your state senator, your state representative, and others who work on those levels of government. Each of us has an obligation to pray for these men and women, by name, on a regular basis.

But you can apply these same principles to your prayers for spiritual leaders on all levels—from your local pastor and church staff members to regional leaders, national leaders, and anyone who oversees an aspect of spiritual life in the Church.

And you can also pray for marketplace leaders, for the "elders" who "sit at the gates" of your city, for those who drive the commerce where you live. In ancient Middle Eastern cities, this was literally the case. A city would have more than one gate, and they were connected by broad walls (which you could compare to the "walls of salvation). At least three offices would be represented or contained at the gateways of a city: commercial, judicial, and prophetic. Actual real estate transactions were handled at the gateway; deeds were transferred; signatures were collected. Court cases and judicial hearings were held right in the gate, and decisions would be announced right there. In addition, prophetic words, the word of the Lord, would be delivered to the priests in the gate (see Prov. 1:21; Jer. 17:19-20; 26:10-13). So there at the gate, a person would find commerce moving, the justice system operating, and spiritual dynamics taking place.

When you pray for those in authority, you are selecting, by name if possible, people who oversee certain spheres and assignments. You have to keep in mind the fact that the spheres of authority are different from each other. If you're praying that an election will be handled with integrity, you'll be praying for the election officials as much as you will the candidates. But those prayers will have little to do with the policies in your local school system—which are decided by school officials. If you want to pray for your local schools, pray for the authorities over the school system. Stick with the right "fields," and pray with the level of faith that God has granted to you (see Rom. 12:3) so that you can bring in a bigger harvest in prayer.

Another angle from which you can approach your prayers is to consider the selection process. Not all people in authority are selected by a vote. Many are appointed, or they grow into their role gradually. For most of them, it is a career or a job. You can pray, based on Deuteronomy 1:13-15, that the wisest and best people will be selected for each job:

> *"Choose wise and discerning and experienced men from your tribes, and I will appoint them as your heads." You* [the people] *answered me* [Moses] *and said, "The thing which you have said to do is good." So I took the heads of your tribes, wise and experienced men, and appointed them heads over you, leaders of thousands and of hundreds, of fifties and of tens, and officers for your tribes* (Deuteronomy 1:13-15).

Very early in colonial America, in 1638, a pastor named Thomas Hooker, preached a sermon in Hartford, Connecticut, based on this passage, and his sermon inspired the creation of the Fundamental Orders of Connecticut, the first written constitution in Western history, which created a government from which the government of the United States can trace its lineal descent. In his sermon, Hooker "forcefully asserted that the choice of public magistrates belongs to the people, that the privilege of election belongs to the people, and that those who have the power to appoint officers of government have the right to limit the power they hold."[4] Thomas Hooker's sermon concluded with the words, "As God hath spared our lives, and given us them in liberty, so to seek the guidance of God, and to choose in God and for God."[5]

In general, biblical principles had a strong influence on those who established the United States of America. Later, Daniel Webster (1782–1852) wrote: "If we abide by the principles taught in the Bible, our country will go on prospering... but if we neglect its instructions and authority, no man can tell how sudden a catastrophe may overwhelm us and bury all of our glory in profound obscurity."[6] In other words, when you pray for people in authority who are selected by others, you may decide to pray first for those who are doing the voting or selecting. Pray that they—including yourself—will abide by biblical principles, will have discernment, wisdom, and integrity, and will be blessed by God in the execution of the tasks that lead up to the selection of new leaders. Pray using biblical terms and principles, combining the always-renewing power of the Word with the fact that much of our governmental system was established by godly people according to biblical principles.

Also, our participation in the voting process is an adjunct to our prayers in a very real way. Voting can be our "works" that are supposed to match our faith. The Book of James tells us that faith without works is dead. "Thus also faith by itself, if it does not have works, is dead" (James 2:17 NKJV). Praying is vital, but it can't stand alone.

What Should You Pray For?

We learn from many Scriptures that God exalts rulers and people in authority if they exercise their authority with righteousness. Proverbs expresses it best: "Righteousness exalts a nation, but sin is a disgrace to any people" (Prov. 14:34), and "If a king judges the poor with truth, his throne will be established forever" (Prov. 29:14).

So one of the first things that we should pray for is that the authority figure will become righteous and will express righteousness, wisdom, and justice in all that he or she does. I pray for those in authority (by name) that they will have God's heart. Often, I use Scripture passages as the basis for my prayers. I often pray something like this:

"Lord, make the President's heart like a channel of water in your hand. Turn it where you wish" (see Prov. 21:1). "Lord, help [a local civil judge] judge the poor with truth and integrity and compassion" (see Prov. 29:14; Ps. 25:21; 2 Cor. 1:3-4). "Father, make it possible for [name of political leader] to humble himself and turn to you and become righteous, for the sake of [the area of the leader's oversight]" (see 2 Chron. 7:14).

Dr. Charles Stanley, pastor of the First Baptist Church in Atlanta, Georgia, along with several other leaders, has suggested ten ways to pray for the men and women who occupy the highest offices in the United States:

1. Pray that they would realize their personal sinfulness and their daily need for cleansing of their sin by Jesus Christ.

2. Pray that they would recognize their personal inadequacy to fulfill their tasks and that they would depend upon God for knowledge, wisdom, and the courage to do what is right.

3. Pray that they would reject all counsel that violates spiritual principles, trusting God to prove them right.

4. Pray that they would resist those who would pressure them to violate their conscience.

5. Pray that they would reverse the trends of socialism and humanism in this nation, both of which deify man rather than God.

6. Pray that they would be ready to sacrifice their personal ambitions and political careers for the sake of this nation, if yielding them would be in the best interest of their country.

7. Pray that they would rely upon prayer and the Word of God as the source of their daily strength, wisdom, and courage.

8. Pray that they would restore dignity, honor, trustworthiness and righteousness to the office they hold.

9. Pray that they would remember to be good examples in their conduct to the fathers, mothers, sons, and daughters of this nation.

10. Pray that they would be reminded daily that they are accountable to Almighty God for the decisions they make.[7]

How else can we pray? Dick Eastman, the president of Every Home for Christ, suggests using three key Scriptures:

1. Proverbs 28:2: "When a country is rebellious, it has many rulers, but a man of understanding and knowledge maintains order" (NIV). See also Isaiah 11:1-3. (Pray for leaders to have knowledge and understanding, which is more than mere information; it includes a grasp of history, roles, cultures, and God's will.)

2. Second Kings 19:28: "Because of your raging against Me, and because your arrogance has come up to My ears, therefore I will put My

hook in your nose, and My bridle in your lips, and I will turn you back by the way which you came." (Pray that God will deal with tyrants, for the sake of His people. Pray that He will hedge in such leaders with limits and boundaries.)

3. Micah 6:8: "He has shown you, O man, what is good; and what does the Lord require of you but to do justly, to love mercy, and to walk humbly with your God?" (NKJV). (Pray that leaders will govern honestly, humbly, and with mercy.)[8]

RESOURCES FOR PRAYING FOR THOSE IN AUTHORITY

In this chapter, I have attempted to furnish you with a basic perspective about praying for people who are in positions of authority as well as to give you some practical ideas. One of the most practical ideas of all is simply to join with others in your praying; this is simply the best way to become more effective in your intercessory prayers. Prayer Storm, of course, is one such coalition of praying believers. Besides Prayer Storm, you may want to connect with one of the ministries listed in Appendix C, "Resources for Intercession."

When it comes to praying specifically for those in governmental authority, I would particularly recommend the National Day of Prayer (www.ndptf.org), which occurs in May under the authority of the President of the United States, the National Governmental Prayer Alliance (www.nationalgpa.org), established by Dutch Sheets, and Intercessors For America (www.ifapray.org), headed up by Gary Bergel. IFA partners with many other organizations, and you can find links to their Web sites on the IFA site, including the sites for America's National Prayer Committee, The U.S. Prayer Center, Mission

America, and others that may be of particular interest to Prayer Storm intercessors who are shouldering the burden of praying for people who are in positions of authority and decision-making within the United States government.

While we each have special prayer assignments, we are all called to pray for people who are in authority. (Review First Timothy 2:1-4.) It is God's heart! It is God's Word! It is God's command! So why don't we just stop turning the pages of this book for a minute and tune in to God's heart, praying for leaders and the issues that concern them?

Father, in accordance with Your Word, we pause and pray for kings and for those in authority. We bring before You the one who is the president of the United States at this time. We pray that You will raise up godly counsel around the president's life, and we pray that the voices of advisors that are based on an unbiblical framework will be silenced. We ask You to provide wisdom like that of Solomon, as well as purity, protection, and safety. We release the knowledge of God's will with all spiritual wisdom and understanding. We also pray for our governor [name your state governor] and for our members of congress on the national and state levels. We pray for those in authority in the judicial system, especially the nine Supreme Court justices of the United States. We bless them in the name of the Lord of hosts.

We pray that all of those in authority would realize and recognize their personal inadequacy to fulfill their role and that You would release to them a revelation of dependency upon God. We pray that You would reverse the trends of socialism and humanism in this nation, because they deify man rather than God.

Lord, as this nation and different nations enter critical times of elections, we call forth those who are truly appointed by You. Let them rise to the top with favor, as cream rises to the top of the milk. Give them a voice that will be heard. Release favor to righteous men and women and to those who are humble, to those who are wise and have revelatory activity upon their lives—release them into positions of influence, impact, and authority. We pray for priorities to be released and for revelation to come about the honor of being a public servant. We pray that there would be a reliance upon the Word of God, the will of God, and the ways of God as the source of daily strength, wisdom, and courage. We pray that there would be a restoration of dignity and honor, of trustworthiness and righteousness in the land.

We pray for our spiritual leaders. We pray for our pastors, our apostles, our prophets, our evangelists, our pastors, and our teachers. We pray blessings and protection over them. We pray for purity. We pray for the quality of life in their families.

We bless those in authority this day, and we declare that this is good and acceptable in the sight of God, our Savior who desires all men and women to be saved and come to the knowledge of the truth. We thank You in Yeshua's great name. Amen.

Canticle of Moses

(The antiphonal prayer below has been rendered in beautiful calligraphy, framed, and hung in our Prayer Room at Encounters Network. This is one of the ancient prayers for Israel long before she was ever re-gathered as a nation in modern history. It was used for 300 years in Bangor, Ireland, during antiphonal worship and prayer.)

Hear, you heavens, the things I speak. Listen, O earth, to the words I say:

Let My teaching drop as rain; let My speech flow down as dew, as a shower on the herbs, as a drop upon the grass. For the name of the Lord I will proclaim. Oh, praise this greatness of our God! The works of God are perfect, and all His ways are just.

Hear, you heavens, the things I speak. Listen, O earth, to the words I say.

God is faithful and does no wrong; He is just and right. Some have sinned against Him, and no longer are His children. They are wicked and perverse. O foolish and unwise people, is this the way you treat Your God, Your Father, Your Creator, who made and formed you?

Hear, you heavens, the things I speak. Listen, O earth, to the words I say.

Remember the days of old! Ask your father, and he will tell you. Ask your elders, and they will explain to you. God divided up the world among the nations, and assigned to each of them a guardian angel, but He Himself took care of Israel.

Hear, you heavens, the things I speak. Listen, O earth, to the words I say.

In a desert land He found Him, in a place of horror and of vast wilderness, He shielded Him and cared for Him; he guarded Him as the apple of His eye.

Hear, you heavens, the things I speak. Listen, O earth, to the words I say.[1]

Chapter 12

PRAYING EFFECTIVELY FOR ISRAEL

Sing with gladness for Jacob, and shout among the chief of the nations; proclaim, give praise, and say, "O Lord, save Your people, the remnant of Israel"(Jeremiah 31:7 NKJV).

Prayer for Israel is one of the four key emphases of Prayer Storm. Because it is so important, I want to give you as much as possible, in an inspiring and equipping manner. I could write whole books about this—and I have (*Praying for Israel's Destiny* and others), and yet, even if you have read the other books, you will find that this chapter will contain some additional insights with a fresh emphasis.

Prayer Storm must raise up *effective* prayer for Israel. The apostle James told us that "...the effectual fervent prayer of a righteous man availeth much" (James 5:16 KJV). That word, *effectual* (or *effective*, in modern translations) is, in Greek, *energeo*, and it implies something that has worked in you and that is, therefore, more effective.[2] It is vital to get beyond dutiful, rote repetition in our prayers, even repetition of Scriptural prayers, and to tap into the recesses of God's heart as you pray.

So the most effective prayers are those that are not merely right information. A parrot can do that. A parrot repeats little phrases, and that's nice, but we want to do better than that. We want to have information plus revelation from God's mind and heart worked into our minds and hearts. *Then* we will be able to really pray. Then our prayers will hit the mark. So let's look at what it means to pray fervent, *effective* prayer for Israel.

PROCLAIM, PRAISE, AND PRAY

As we read in the passage from Jeremiah, at the beginning of this chapter, God's clear command to us is to "proclaim, give praise, and say [pray], 'O Lord, save Thy people, the remnant of Israel'" (Jer. 31:7 NKJV). These are our biblical mandates.

In order to proclaim, give praise, and pray effectively, we need to review the biblical history of Israel, focusing in particular on *aliyah* (the "ascent," or "return to the land"), which is so foundational to understanding Israel's future. We need to read passages such as Jeremiah 31:8-10 with fresh eyes:

> *"Behold, I am bringing them from the north country, and I will gather them from the remote parts of the earth, among them the blind and the lame, the woman with child and she who is in labor with child, together; a great company, they will return here. With weeping they will come, and by supplication I will lead them; I will make them walk by streams of waters, on a straight path in which they will not stumble; for I am a father to Israel, and Ephraim is My firstborn." Hear the word of the Lord, O nations, and declare in the coastlands afar off, and say, "He who scattered Israel will gather him and keep him as a shepherd keeps his flock"* (Jeremiah 31:8-10).

How will the descendents of Abraham be led back together to the land of Israel? *"By supplication."* Whose supplication? Yours and mine! They will be led back, and already have been led back, to the land as a result of the prayers of God's people.

Where will they come from? "From the north country" and "from the remote parts of the earth." On the wings of prayer, these words have been fulfilled repeatedly in our day, especially since the establishment of the State of Israel in 1948. I save newspaper clippings that tell some of the stories, such as "Solomon's Flight," when 14,500 Ethiopian Jews returned during the administration of George H.W. Bush.[3]

What should we pray for? We should proclaim the will of God for His people, praise Him for every step and new development, and pray without ceasing for God's blessing on *aliyah* and His protection ("as a shepherd keeps his flock") for the people who have come back to their ancestral land.

Why should we pray this way? Partially it is because the *land* itself, within the boundaries of Israel, is where God will reveal Himself to His people as their Messiah. God's message rings loud and clear in these Scriptures:

Yet the number of the sons of Israel will be like the sand of the sea, which cannot be measured or numbered; and in the place where it is said to them, "You are not My people," it will be said to them, "You are the sons of the living God" (Hosea 1:10).

"Therefore behold, days are coming," declares the Lord, "when it will no longer be said, 'As the Lord lives, who brought up the sons of Israel out of the land of Egypt,' but, 'As the Lord lives, who brought up the sons of Israel from the land of the north and from all the countries where He had banished them.' For I will restore them to their own land which I gave to their fathers" (Jeremiah 16:14-15).

"Therefore behold, the days are coming," declares the Lord, "when they will no longer say, 'As the Lord lives, who brought up the sons of Israel from the land of Egypt,' but,

'As the Lord lives, who brought up and led back the descendants of the household of Israel from the north land and from all the countries where I had driven them.' Then they will live on their own soil" (Jeremiah 23:7-8).

Then it will happen on that day that the Lord will again recover the second time with His hand the remnant of His people....And He will...assemble the banished ones of Israel, and will gather the dispersed of Judah from the four corners of the earth (Isaiah 11:11-12).

Do not fear, for I am with you; I will bring your offspring from the east, and gather you from the west. I will say to the north, "Give them up!" and to the south, "Do not hold them back." Bring My sons from afar and My daughters from the ends of the earth (Isaiah 43:5-6).

"For behold, days are coming," declares the Lord, "when I will restore the fortunes of My people Israel and Judah." The Lord says, "I will also bring them back to the land that I gave to their forefathers and they shall possess it" (Jeremiah 30:3).

It's the *place*, you see. It is vital to understand that the soil of Israel is where God wants to gather the remnant of His people so that He can restore their inheritance and become their Shepherd-King. And it is important to notice, in Isaiah 11:11, for example, that this will be a *re*-gathering of the people. "The Lord will again recover the *second* time...." This is borne out historically. First there was a gathering in of the remnant of Israel from specific regions and countries. The Jewish people of many other countries, whose ancestors had been dispersed there generations before, were unaffected. In the present day, the Jewish people are being gathered from every part of the globe: "He…will gather the dispersed of Judah from the four corners of the earth" (Isa. 11:12).

An enormous amount has already happened. People have returned to the land in wave after wave. From 1989 to 2007, 1.3 million Jews made *aliyah* from the "land of the north" (the former Soviet Union). I have been told by several sources that, at this point, there are more than 1.3 million Russian-speaking Jews in Israel, and Russian is now the second leading spoken language in Israel.

Most of us are very familiar, from listening to daily media reports, with the fact that, though making *aliyah* means reaching the Promised Land, it is far from "Heaven on earth." Peace is fragile; threats are real. Sadly, suicide bombers are relentless, and attacks with short-range missiles from all sides are constant. Only the ongoing prayers of the Church around the world will ensure that Israel is protected and that her prophetic destiny is fulfilled.

UNDERSTANDING GOD'S MYSTERIOUS PLAN FOR ISRAEL

There are three things that we must grasp in order to discover God's desire to awaken love in our hearts for the Jewish people. The apostle Paul calls this a "mystery":

For I do not want you, brethren, to be uninformed of this mystery—so that you will not be wise in your own estimation—that a partial hardening has happened to Israel until the fullness of the Gentiles has come in; and so all Israel will be saved; just as it is written, "The Deliverer will come from Zion, He will remove ungodliness from Jacob. This is my covenant with them, when I take away their sins." From the standpoint of the gospel they are enemies for your sake, but from the standpoint of God's choice they are beloved for the sake of the fathers; for the gifts and the calling of God are irrevocable. For just as you once were disobedient to God, but now have been shown mercy because of their disobedience, so these also now have been disobedient, that because of the mercy shown to you they also may now be shown mercy. For God has shut up all in disobedience so that He may show mercy to all (Romans 11:25-32).

The three things we must grasp from this passage are as follows. I will explain each of them below:

1. All Israel at some point will be saved and brought to fullness.

2. The Jewish people have a spirit of blindness as it relates to seeing their Messiah.

3. The blinders of the Jewish people will be removed when "the fullness of the Gentiles" is ushered in.

All Israel Saved

All Israel will be saved and brought to fullness. Before Jesus returns to rule over the earth, He will release a spirit of prayer (supplication) and demonstrations of His amazing saving grace that will cause the Jewish people who have survived the antichrist's rage to come to full faith. As Paul wrote to the Romans, "All Israel will be saved" (Rom. 11:26). They will be overwhelmed with a deep spirit of repentance. Look at Zechariah's prophetic words:

And I will pour on the house of David and on the inhabitants of Jerusalem the Spirit of grace and supplication; then they will look on Me whom they pierced. Yes, they will mourn for Him as one mourns for his only son, and grieve for Him as one grieves for a firstborn. In that day there shall be a great mourning in Jerusalem, like the mourning at Hadad Rimmon in the plain of Megiddo (Zechariah 12:10-11 NKJV).

Prayer will cause their blinders to come off, and it will cause their hearts to be softened. Why can't this happen earlier? God has a timetable for all strategic events. God is in charge of the clock. Although we are hearing about fresh stirrings of the Holy Spirit among the Jewish people in Israel and elsewhere, we must recognize that God will save the "best wine" (see John 2:10) for a last, dynamic outpouring, which will occur at the end of the age. Paul's letter to the Romans describes this as "fullness," calling it "life from the dead." (See Romans 11:12,15 NIV.) Israel is being and will be awakened!

Paul's primary purpose in writing to the churches in Rome was to make them aware that God's call, promises, and covenants concerning Israel's redemptive purposes were (and are) still in effect, even if the majority of the Jewish population was (and is) oblivious to their God-ordained destiny. Paul, writing to the Romans, who were predominantly Gentiles, received from God a revelation of God's end-time purposes for the final, greatest revival of all time, and the key element of it is that all of Israel will be saved!

Blind Toward Their Messiah

The Jewish people have a spirit of blindness as it relates to seeing their Messiah. Aren't you glad that, when you wore blinders, God had a plan for your life? Just as He had mercy on you, He wants to lavish His loving mercy on His chosen ones. When the time fully comes, the blinders will come off, and the Jews will "look on Him whom they have pierced and weep"— along with the rest of us. I want to be careful to emphasize the fact that the sin of *all* of mankind crucified Jesus, not just the sin of one group of people, the Jews. We must be very clear on that, because Christian history has been fouled by episodes of rage against the Jewish people for something that we all must take responsibility for. It is the sin of mankind, past, present, and future, that the Father purposefully laid on the Son.

For the past 2,000 years, the Gentiles have been able to take their blinders off, becoming believers in the Messiah and, therefore, God's "primary" instrument for the establishment of His Kingdom, working to bring the Gospel to all nations before the Second Coming of Christ. But it is absolutely vital to note that Israel's rejection of Jesus is neither total nor final (see Rom. 11:1-32). The diagnosis: they have a temporary spirit of blindness as it relates to seeing their Messiah.

It is the ignorance of the Church that has led many to wrongly conclude that God has rejected Israel and that Israel, therefore, has no future role to play. They believe that Israel has disqualified herself and that the predominately Gentile Church will play the central role in God's redemptive plans both now and throughout eternity.

We find ourselves in a dilemma. The current dilemma is that the Jewish people are mostly blind and that Gentile believers are mostly ignorant when it comes to revelation about God's future plans to raise up and fully restore His original covenant people (see Ezek. 36). However, God has not given up on using Israel as His primary instrument to establish His Kingdom on earth. God remains faithful, even when we are faithless! Thank the Lord!

In order to reverse Israel's current hostility toward their Messiah and the sad history of the Church, something drastic must take place. Jesus called this period (the great tribulation) the worst period that the earth will ever experience (see Matt. 24:21-22). The prophet Jeremiah called it "Jacob's trouble" (see Jer. 30:7). Daniel described it as the most difficult time ever (see Dan. 12:1).

Where will they turn? Because of the desperation of the times, true compassionate Gentile believers will rise up in prayer and supplication, and mighty waves of God's mercy will flow in the Land of Promise. There will be an awakening in Israel! Yes, there will be a revival of kindness in the Church!

The Fullness of the Gentiles

The blinders of the Jewish people will be removed when "the fullness of the Gentiles" is ushered in. In other words, the "fullness of the Gentiles" will usher in the "fullness of the Jewish people" (see Rom. 11:25-26).

The phrase *the fullness of the Gentiles* has several dimensions. First, it refers to the full number of Gentile converts written in the Lamb's Book of Life (see Rev. 7:9; 21:27). The term *fullness* also signifies the unprecedented release of the Holy Spirit's power at the end of the age, which will result in a harvest of souls unsurpassed in human history. This historic revival will have an impact on every nation on the earth. That is why we must pray, in our weekly Prayer Storm efforts, for revival in the Church and for the greatest youth awakening that the world has ever seen!

God's plan is to use believers who are walking in obedience and wholehearted consecration, believers who carry a burden for the Jewish people. God will use their extreme commitment to Him, coupled with their servant hearts toward Israel and all the descendants of Abraham, to win many Jews, Arabs, Chaldeans, and residents of the Middle East to His Son, the

Messiah. He wants to bring both Jew and Gentile into the full knowledge of Him so that "the earth will be filled with the knowledge of the glory of the Lord, as the waters cover the sea" (Hab. 2:14).

STANDING WITH THE JEWISH PEOPLE—THE CHURCH'S CALL

The Church, which is largely Gentile, must stand firmly with the Jewish people, because one of God's primary strategies to win the hearts of the Jewish people is through a compassionate and faithful Gentile Church. Paul—himself once a zealous Jew and then the greatest spokesman for God's heart toward the Jews in his letter to the Romans—defined the Gentiles' call as "provoking them to jealousy" (see Rom. 11:11 NKJV). This simply means that, when the Gentile Church begins to walk in authentic, compassionate spiritual authority, the Kingdom shining through them will be extremely inviting and attractive to the Jewish people, which in turn will cause them to desire a deeper relationship with God by receiving their Messiah as their Savior.

Jesus made a strong appeal to the Gentile believers to not forsake His Jewish people during their times of great trouble when He described the time of judgment. (See Matthew 25:31-42.) The Jewish people must be included in "the least of these," who were hungry, thirsty, lonely, naked, sick, or in prison when the righteous ones helped them. Those who choose to disregard that appeal and the urgings of their consciences will suffer the consequences of being numbered with the "goat nations."

Throughout his letter to the Roman church, Paul warned his readers about the consequences of being spiritually ignorant and therefore arrogant—and potentially apostate.

But if some of the branches were broken off, and you, being a wild olive, were grafted in among them and became partaker with them of the rich root of the olive tree, do not be arrogant toward the branches; but if you are arrogant, remember that it is not you who supports the root, but the root supports you. You will say then, "Branches were broken off so that I might be grafted in." Quite right, they were broken off for their unbelief, but you stand by your faith. Do not be conceited, but fear; for if God did not spare the natural branches, He will not spare you, either. Behold then the kindness and severity of God; to those who fell, severity, but to you, God's kindness, if you continue in His kindness; otherwise you also will be cut off (Romans 11:17-22).

Paul showed us what can happen when we take this matter lightly. Left unattended, ignorance leads to arrogance, which eventually can lead to spiritual apostasy. This was one of the greatest burdens on Paul's heart:

I am telling the truth in Christ, I am not lying, my conscience testifies with me in the Holy Spirit, that I have great sorrow and unceasing grief in my heart. For I could wish that I myself were accursed, separated from Christ for the sake of my brethren, my kinsmen according to the flesh, who are Israelites, to whom belongs the adoption as sons, and the glory and the covenants and the giving of the Law and the temple service and the promises, whose are the fathers, and from whom is the Christ according to the flesh, who is over all... (Romans 9:1-5).

PRAYING FOR THE PEACE OF JERUSALEM

Praying for the peace of Jerusalem is God's desire and His call to everyone, to the entire Church throughout the world:

I was glad when they said to me, "Let us go into the house of the Lord." Our feet have been standing within your gates, O Jerusalem! Jerusalem is built as a city that is compact together, where the tribes go up, the tribes of the Lord, to the Testimony of Israel, to give thanks to the name of the Lord. For thrones are set there for judgment, the thrones of the house of David. Pray for the peace of Jerusalem: "May they prosper who love you. Peace be within your walls, prosperity within your palaces." For the sake of my brethren and companions, I will now say, "Peace be within you." Because of the house of the Lord our God I will seek your good (Psalm 122 NKJV).

Through the prophet Isaiah, God commanded His people to "give Him no rest" until Jerusalem enters into the fullness of her inheritance: "I have set watchmen on your walls, O Jerusalem; they shall never hold their peace day or night. You who make mention of the Lord, do not keep silent, and give Him no rest till He establishes and till He makes Jerusalem a praise in the earth" (Isa. 62:6-7 NKJV).

The *peace of Jerusalem* refers to Israel entering into the fullness of her destiny as spoken by the Old Testament prophets. You can see here that God is calling the Body of the Messiah to give herself in fervent intercession for the salvation of the inhabitants of a dusty Middle Eastern city that is likely the most contention-filled place on the face of the earth. He wants peace there! He wants His Kingdom to come there! He wants the Church—which is you and me—to stand with Him, with His Word, with His ways, and with His heart.

Praying for Jerusalem puts you in partnership with the heart of God. His heart is consumed with zeal for this city. You and I want to be where He is. Where is He? He is watching over this city. With Him, we watch and pray for Jerusalem. This piece of real estate is not insignificant, nor has it lost its chance to attract His attention. Again, here is the cry of His heart:

> *Thus says the Lord of hosts, "I am exceedingly jealous for Jerusalem and Zion. But I am very angry with the nations who are at ease; for while I was only a little angry, they furthered the disaster." Therefore thus says the Lord, "I will return to Jerusalem with compassion; My house will be built in it," declares the Lord of hosts, "and a measuring line will be stretched over Jerusalem"* (Zechariah 1:14-16).

> *For Zion's sake I will not keep silent, and for Jerusalem's sake I will not keep quiet, until her righteousness goes forth like brightness, and her salvation like a torch that is burning* (Isaiah 62:1).

When we pray for Jerusalem, we are contending for the salvation of the people of Israel. As we have already noted, Israel's acceptance of Jesus as her Messiah depends upon her being provoked to jealousy by a predominantly Gentile Church (see Rom. 11:11), and God's strategy is to show mercy through the Gentile Body of believers (see Rom. 11:30-32). Part of showing mercy to Israel is standing in the place of prayer for Jerusalem.

We want to see Jesus' return as their Messiah, but His return is contingent upon Israel's acceptance of Him as such. Jesus said it loud and clear:

> *O Jerusalem, Jerusalem, you who kill the prophets and stone those sent to you, how often I have longed to gather your children together, as a hen gathers her chicks under her wings, but you were not willing. Look, your house is left to you desolate. For I tell you, **you will not see Me again until you say, "Blessed is He who comes in the name of the Lord"*** (Matthew 23:37-39 NIV).

Right away, in the days following Pentecost, Peter and the new Church of Jesus Christ started calling the nation of Israel and the leading figures of Jerusalem to repent and to put their faith in Jesus so that "your sins may be blotted out,...and that He may send Jesus Christ, who was preached to you before" (Acts 3:19-20 NKJV).

Right away also, satan launched an all-out assault on the nation of Israel and the city of Jerusalem. He knows that Jesus committed Himself to returning as King of the Jews, to rule the earth from Jerusalem (see Matt. 23:39). Satan heard Him with his own ears. If satan can annihilate the Jewish people, he can prove God to be a liar and ensure his own survival. So he attempts to rally the nations of the earth to his cause. Global anti-Semitism is the result. In our own lifetimes, we may see the time when every nation of the earth actively seeks the destruction of Jerusalem under the leadership of a world leader commonly known as the antichrist. (See First John 4:3; Zechariah 12:2; 14:2, and Zephaniah 3:7-8.)

As the saints of God partner with Him in prayer and in solidarity with Israel, He promises to do two things in response:

1. He will release His voice in the earth (the "spirit of prophecy"). The spirit of prophecy is the testimony of Jesus (see Rev. 19:10). The testimony of Jesus results in revival among the Gentiles, which will provoke Israel to jealousy.

2. He will release supernatural activity in the earth (judgments against His enemies). He wants righteousness to prevail (see Isa. 62:1-2), and He will raise up messengers who will proclaim with boldness, authority, and clarity the "Gospel of the Kingdom" (see Matt. 24:14), especially to the Jewish people in the midst of tribulation. He

will release signs and wonders as evidence of His coming again (see Joel 2:30-31).

Salvation and Deliverance in Jerusalem

Do you see this? Praying for the peace of Jerusalem means that you're praying for Israel to come into her fullness—which means that you're also praying for the Gentiles' fullness, because it will cause Israel's fullness. So praying for Jerusalem and for Israel means that you're also praying for the end-time, progressive purposes of God to unfold for all people across the entire planet.

So often, people don't get this. They think that praying for Jerusalem is optional. But it's an integral part of the end-time harvest. It all adds together. God's end-time activity is released out of His zeal for Jerusalem. The end result—the deliverance of Jerusalem from her enemies, the salvation of all Israel, and the establishment of God's Kingdom on the earth in fullness (see Rom. 11:26-27)—comes because of God's people lining up with His heart and praying for the salvation of Israel with fasting, solemn assemblies, and midnight watches:

> Blow a trumpet in Zion, consecrate a fast, proclaim a solemn assembly, gather the people, sanctify the congregation, assemble the elders, gather the children and the nursing infants. Let the bridegroom come out of his room and the bride out of her bridal chamber. Let the priests, the Lord's ministers, weep between the porch and the altar, and let them say, "Spare Your people, O Lord, and do not make Your inheritance a reproach, a byword among the nations" (Joel 2:15-17).

One of the ultimate tasks of the Gentile Church is to pray for the salvation of Israel, yearning for the Jews to be included in the Kingdom and to receive the mercy of God. That is why, in our Prayer Storm, we're going to partner with the other fasting and prayer movements and initiatives that God has raised up. That is why we host The Cry each year—three days of prayer and fasting for Israel during the time of Purim (see Appendix B for more details).

Ever since 1967, when, as a result of war in the Middle East, Jerusalem was once again brought under the control of the Jewish people and became the state of Israel, the dispensation of the Gentiles began to shift in a significant way. It's coming into focus. In the midst of all the confusion and the contentiousness, we can see that Jerusalem is becoming the last-days epicenter for God's activity in the earth. You must always remember, Israel is still the apple of God's eye (see Zech. 2:8)! When you can grasp this with your eyes and heart, and when you join your voice and your efforts with others, you become an end-time harvester. O let the spirit of prayer consume you as it has me! Join with me now in praying.

> *Father, I want You to give me Your heart for Israel and the Jewish people worldwide. Give me the spirit of grace and supplication so that I can join others who are effective watchmen on the walls for such a time as this. Count me in! I want to partner with You for Israel's salvation, and I want to help stand in the gap in times of crisis. I want to see the glory of God flood the entire Middle East. May Your prophetic purposes come forth in this generation for all the descendants of Abraham, for Your Holy name's sake. In Yeshua's great name. Amen and Amen!*

Conclusion

THE CHALLENGE

[Of the mighty men who helped King David were] the sons of Issachar, men who understood the times, with knowledge of what Israel should do, their chiefs were two hundred; and all their kinsmen were at their command (1 Chronicles 12:32).

As I described at the beginning of this book, God used a vivid dream to show me the vision and outline for Prayer Storm. It was a powerfully compelling experience. A little later, God began to confirm the words He had shown me. God will always confirm His Word by the testimony of two or three (or more) witnesses—believers like you and me. He wants us to know that His Word is true and can be "banked on."

I considered it pure confirmation when I heard about another dream. Julie Meyer, who is a friend of many years and a recording artist, prophetess, and singer at the International House of Prayer in Kansas City, had a dream about a major storm arising and the response of the people of God. It emphasized the necessity of properly interpreting the revelations we receive.

In January 2008, at our annual Encounters Network Secret Place Gathering in Franklin, Tennessee, Julie sang this dream to me, prophetically. With great clarity, she declared from Ezekiel 1:4 (the same Scripture with which I opened Chapter 1) that the Lord is mounting a prayer storm that will be huge. Her song was a confirmation that a prayer storm will arise across the nations and that we have a part to play in it.

Here is the dream Julie received, as she recorded it in her book, *Invitation to Encounter: A Journey in Dreams*. Julie has given me permission to share it with you.

A Storm Is Coming

The sons of Issachar knew the signs of the times and what to do (1 Chron. 12:32). Whenever we see signs, we need to ask God what He is saying so that we can interpret them correctly and not become caught up with the signs themselves.

I had a dream. I was at a gathering that felt like a big family celebration. My children were there, and others had brought their children as well. Most of the people attending served in positions of leadership: worship leaders and team members, small-group leaders, teachers, and the like.

All of a sudden, a gentle breeze began to blow and get increasingly stronger. There was a huge five-by-five-foot picture window that rattled as the wind intensified. The rattling got my attention and, as I looked around the room, I noticed that others were also beginning to pay attention.

I looked out through the window and saw that new colors had overtaken the sky. Instead of white clouds, I saw large crimson clouds and bright green clouds. They were tumbling and billowing and burning bright. It was startling.

> Then I looked, and behold, a whirlwind was coming out of the north, a great cloud with raging fire engulfing itself; and brightness was all around it and radiating out of its midst like the color of amber, out of the midst of the fire (Ezekiel 1:4).

We were awestruck by the breathtaking beauty of the contrasting colors. We stood in silence, marveling at the clouds and wondering what this sight could mean. After a few moments, each person began quoting various Scriptures as they strained to give meaning to the sign.

"The heavens declare the glory of God…The Son is the radiance of God's glory…The grace of God that brings salvation has appeared to all men…The righteousness of God extends to the clouds…Do not put out the Spirit's fire…Jesus Christ will be glorified in his holy people and marveled at by all those who have believed."

Though each Scripture was a true statement, God was saying something different. They were so caught up in the sign itself that they missed its true meaning: a storm was coming. Fearful dread—the raw fear of the Lord—suddenly gripped me because I knew none of them had interpreted the sign correctly.

Next to me stood a man who was like a son of Issachar. He was seasoned in leadership and had great prophetic understanding because of his many years spent at the Lord's feet. He shook his head as if to say of the verses everyone had listed, "No, that is not the correct interpretation." In a measured, slow whisper of certainty and sobriety, he explained the sign clearly: *"There is a storm coming. There is a storm coming, Beloved, there is a storm coming."*

Signs are meant to direct us into dialogue with God; they are not an end in themselves. We must look past signs, no matter how great or terrifying they seem, and ask the Lord for the right interpretation.[1]

YES, A STORM IS COMING

There *is* a storm coming. A storm is coming. It's a storm of violence. The sky is filled with supernatural clashes. The war of the Lamb is being waged on a cosmic level, and we are some of His end-time players on His stage of history. Are you prepared? Are you wide awake? Are you properly interpreting what the Holy Spirit is saying in this hour?

The watchmen have been anticipating this storm. They are ready for it. They have assembled themselves into an army of watchers who fast and pray for the Kingdom of God to come across the earth. They are part of a long line of watchmen prayer-warriors who have been pressing forward relentlessly for centuries. They can recognize each other from afar. Over there are the sixth-century monks in Bangor, Ireland. Nearby are the 18th-century Moravians in Hernnhut, Germany. Right here and now are the 21st-century 24/7 prayer rooms. And here is Prayer Storm, praying hour after hour for revival in the Church, a great youth awakening, Israel, and major crises all over the world.

The hearts of the watchers are as tender toward Jesus as a bride's heart is tender toward her bridegroom. Filled with the Holy Spirit, they grow closer to God's heart as they pray. Sometimes they fast—their hearts are lovesick, and they cannot sacrifice enough for Him. After all, He is worthy. He alone is worthy!

CALLED TO PRAY

Most of these intercessors can trace their call to pray back many years. Even before they heard about others interceding or the "hour that changes the world," they yearned to spend time with Jesus in prayerful intimacy. Is this true for you?

In my own life, the Holy Spirit gave me a love and a call long before He gave me a commissioning. When I was a young boy in a little country old time Methodist church, I used to love the Sunday evening "Song Fests." The entire service would be singing. People would shout out what hymn they wanted to sing next by its title or page number in the hymnal. Estyl Bowers would play the piano. Ethel Mae Kilburn, whose physician-husband had attended my birth in my parents' home, would lead the singing with her strong soprano voice.

Imprinted on my memory is the singing of "The Beautiful Garden of Prayer." On one special night, I was nestled in the last row, in the corner of the old oak pew, sitting close to motherly Ida Mae Smith. We sang our hearts out together. We were *in* the beautiful garden of prayer with Him, a place where grace abounds and prayer is a delight, not a chore.

Ever after that Sunday evening, I have sought out "garden moments" with Him. That night, I discovered a secret—to be in His presence in the garden of prayer will calm any storm. The most glorious place on this side of Heaven is to be with Jesus. He makes every place of encounter into a garden sanctuary. Here are the words to this little known hymn. This song is who I am. It is a song of who you are destined to become!

THE BEAUTIFUL GARDEN OF PRAYER

There's a garden where Jesus is waiting,
There's a place that is wondrously fair,
For it glows with the light of His presence.
'Tis the beautiful garden of prayer.

(Refrain) *Oh, the beautiful garden, the garden of prayer!*
Oh, the beautiful garden of prayer!
There my Savior awaits, and He opens the gates
To the beautiful garden of prayer.

There's a garden where Jesus is waiting,
And I go with my burden and care,

Just to learn from His lips words of comfort
In the beautiful garden of prayer.

There's a garden where Jesus is waiting,
And He bids you to come, meet Him there;
Just to bow and receive a new blessing
In the beautiful garden of prayer.[2]

PRAYER STORM—SIGN UP NOW!

To sign up now to become a part of the worldwide Prayer Storm team, go to:

http://prayerstorm.com

click on:

"Sign Up Now."

You will be able to fill out a form with your name, address, and e-mail address. Then you will use a drop-down box to fill out your time zone anywhere in the world, the day of the week you wish to pray for one hour, and the specific hour (your local time) that you wish to pray.

At our Prayer Storm headquarters in Franklin, Tennessee, in the central time zone of the United States, we will keep track of the times and hours and will send you regular communications. You will also be able to view our weekly Prayer Storm webcast where you will welcome me right into your own home, hotel room, or college dorm room through the World Wide Web, and we can spend time interceding together.

Prayer Storm—Praying

- for revival in the Church,
- for Israel and all the descendents of Abraham,

- for the greatest youth awakening the world has ever seen, and

- for crisis intervention through intercession.

The world has had its terrorist attacks, tsunamis, hurricanes, earthquakes, famines, wars and rumors of wars, and other disastrous storms. But there is a Prayer Storm that is arising that is great in force. It is led by a band of relentless believers in the Lord Jesus Christ who will not give up! These nameless and faceless intercessors will only bow their knee to the Lord Jesus Christ. And they are committed to a task—that the Lamb of God be magnified through out all the earth. Like the Moravians who went before them, these Prayer Stormers want Jesus Christ the Lord to receive the reward of His sufferings.

Are you ready to be a part of the "hour that changes the world?"

Heaven is waiting for your reply!

Join me! Join others! Remember, together in Jesus, we make a great team!

With a passion for the Lord Jesus Christ,
James W. Goll

Appendix A

PRAYER STORM
ONE-HOUR PRAYER GUIDE

This guide is intended to be only an outline, surrendered to the leading of the Holy Spirit as a flexible tool to help you in your hour of worship and intercession as part of Prayer Storm. It is not a formula, and you do not have to follow it to the letter. Your times of prayer may vary greatly from one week to the next, as the Spirit leads you. Below, you will find a brief outline, followed by further explanation.

60-MINUTE OUTLINE FOR PRAYER STORM PRAYER

- Read the current Prayer Storm Prayer Alert—2 minutes
- Offer thanksgiving and praise—3 minutes
- Sing and pray in the Spirit—5 minutes
- Read Scripture—5 minutes
- Pray for revival in the Church—10 minutes
- Sing and pray in the Spirit—5 minutes
- Pray for Israel—10 minutes
- Sing and pray in the Spirit—5 minutes
- Pray for a youth awakening—10 minutes
- Offer thanksgiving and praise—5 minutes

A FEW INSTRUCTIONS

Based on this outline, here are a few simple instructions to help you make your time effective.

Weekly Prayer Alerts will be sent out to each Prayer Storm participant. They will be posted also on the Prayer Storm Web site (www.prayerstorm.com). Please begin by reading the current Prayer Alert. Then proceed to offer thanksgiving and praise to the Lord. Remember, Psalm 100 instructs us to enter into His gates with thanksgiving and into His courts with praise. You can enter God's throne room with thanksgiving and praise! If you find music helpful, play an instrument or use an instrumental worship CD in the background. Do whatever will make your time the most effective.

One of the emphases of Prayer Storm is upon Spirit-led and Spirit-empowered worship and prayer. Therefore, consider singing and praying in the Holy Spirit or praying by using the gift of tongues (see 1 Cor. 14) as a part of your time. If you have not yet been released into this dimension of prayer, do not worry. You can participate by simply worshiping the Lord periodically throughout your hour. Remember, the Lord inhabits the praises of His people. You are one of His people, and He will inhabit your praises.

It is vital to be Spirit-led and Word-grounded in your times of intercession. Every so often, the Prayer Alert will direct you to read a Scripture passage that will fuel your faith. At other times, it will be left up to you to select a short portion of the Bible to read.

As you proceed into the current "burdens or themes" in prayer, make it practical. Call out to the Lord for revival in the Church. Pray for your region and nation and the church in your city to come alive in Jesus' name! As you proceed through the theme(s) for that week, remember that the Web site incorporates Scripture-based teaching outlines for every area or emphasis: revival in the Church, prayer for Israel, youth awakening, and crisis intercession. Avail yourself of these tools, as they will help you hit the mark in your prayers.

While the outline lists the different prayer themes in a certain order, giving each subject a few minutes, you should be aware that the Holy Spirit might "land on" one of them, such as revival in the Church, and you will not be able to get away from it. That is great! Follow His lead; that is the goal. Other times, you will not be aware of a particular leading of the Spirit, so you will simply pray through this outline or one that you have devised. Either way is good. Just be faithful in your hourly watch.

Also note that crisis intercession does not appear as a special section in this prayer outline. That is because special notices for crisis intercession will be e-mailed out whenever necessary. Again, there might be times when your entire hour or another day or hour will be spent entirely on crisis intercession. That is wonderful. Intercessors are to be flexible instruments in the Lord's hand.

You will notice that the outline keeps coming back to singing and praying in the Spirit. This is important! Your faith will be charged, and your prayers will then be supernaturally guided if you worship the Lord and pray in the Spirit frequently.

You will also notice that the hour not only begins with thanksgiving and praise, it also ends with it. Thank Him and praise Him for His answers to your prayers. Thank Him and praise Him that He is raising up intercessors all over the globe. Rejoice that the fire of the Moravian lampstand is not going out and that the continuous chorus of prayer is swelling even as you speak. Offer up a shout if you want. Thank the Lord that He has heard you and many other intercessors around the globe who are taking their place as watchmen on the walls for such a time as this.

May these simple guidelines help you to have an effective time in your Prayer Storm assignment!

PRAYER STORM—RESTORING AND RELEASING THE GLOBAL MORAVIAN LAMPSTAND

The fire shall ever be burning upon the altar; it shall never go out (Leviticus 6:13 KJV).

(For an online version of this prayer guide, go to the Prayer Storm website: http://www.prayerstorm.com/1hour_outline. html.)

Appendix B

PURIM PRAYER FOCUS FOR ISRAEL
(The Esther Fast)

In the time of Persia's King Artaxerxes, an evil official named Haman plotted to wipe out the people of Israel in a massacre. Desperate to save her people, Queen Esther, who was a Jew, declared a three-day fast from both food and water, after which she approached the king and, through divine intervention, obtained deliverance from the imminent genocide. You can read the dramatic story in the Book of Esther.

> [Mordecai sent a message that said,] *"For if you remain silent at this time, relief and deliverance will arise for the Jews from another place and you and your father's house will perish. And who knows whether you have not attained royalty for such a time as this?"*
>
> *Then Esther told them to reply to Mordecai, "Go, assemble all the Jews who are found in Susa, and fast for me; do not eat or drink for three days, night or day. I and my maidens also will fast in the same way. And thus I will go in to the king, which is not according to the law; and if I perish, I perish...."*
>
> *Now it came about on the third day that Esther put on her royal robes and stood in the inner court of the king's palace in front of the king's rooms, and the king was sitting on his*

royal throne in the throne room, opposite the entrance to the palace. When the king saw Esther the queen standing in the court, she obtained favor in his sight; and the king extended to Esther the golden scepter which was in his hand. So Esther came near and touched the top of the scepter.

Then the king said to her, "What is troubling you, Queen Esther? And what is your request? Even to half of the kingdom it shall be given to you...."

Now in the twelfth month (that is, the month Adar), on the thirteenth day when the king's command and edict were about to be executed, on the day when the enemies of the Jews hoped to gain the mastery over them, it was turned to the contrary so that the Jews themselves gained the mastery over those who hated them.....This [Jewish victory over their enemies] *was done on the thirteenth day of the month Adar, and on the fourteenth day they rested and made it a day of feasting and rejoicing.* (Esther 4:14-16; 5:1-3, 9:1,17).

To this day, Jews celebrate Purim as a holiday that commemorates God's deliverance of the Jewish people through Esther's courageous actions. On the Jewish calendar, it used to be celebrated on the 14th of Adar in the unwalled cities and on the 15th of Adar in the cities that were walled in the time of Joshua. Today it is celebrated from sunset on the first day through nightfall on the second, and it is preceded by a fast that mirrors Esther's three-day fast.

Because the Church is like a spiritual Esther, many Christian intercessors declare a three-day "Esther fast" at Purim, fasting and seeking God's favor and protection for the Jews and for the overthrow of evil in our day. Desperate times require desperate measures. Purim is a good time to intercede against the plots and schemes of the modern-day spirit of Haman. I call this annual time of fasting and intervention intercession The Cry, and I urge you to consider joining with others who pray at this time in this way. For more information, go to my website at http://www.ministrytothenations.org/israel.html. Below are the dates of the Feast of Purim for the next several years:

Year	Feast of Purim	Esther Fast Dates
2009	March 10	March 8-10
2010	February 28	February 26-28
2011	March 20	March 18-20
2012	March 8	March 6-8
2013	February 24	February 22-24
2014	March 16	March 14-16
2015	March 5	March 3-5
2016	March 24	March 22-24
2017	March 12	March 10-12
2018	March 1	February 27-March 1
2019	March 21	March 19-21
2020	March 10	March 8-10

To undertake a complete Esther Fast, do not eat or drink (except for taking Holy Communion) for the duration of the three days. Do not undertake the Esther fast unless you are in good health and you follow normal guidelines for starting and ending the time of fasting. If necessary, adapt the type of fast to fit your life and schedule. But whatever you do, do it with all your heart!

The purpose of fasting is so that you can devote yourself without reservation to extra prayer and Scripture-reading. Below you will find a list of Scriptures that you might find helpful. Use the Scriptures to guide your prayers, and be specific when you pray. Include prayers for yourself, asking God to direct and empower you in your own ministry in the Body of Christ and praying for reconciliation in your own personal relationships as well as among groups, regions, and nations on the earth. Pray for forgiveness for yourself and also for the sins of your nation as Daniel did (see Dan. 9). These psalms provide an excellent framework for prayer for national forgiveness:

> *Hear my prayer, O Lord! And let my cry for help come to You. Do not hide Your face from me in the day of my distress; incline Your ear to me; in the day when I call answer me quickly.... You will arise and have compassion on Zion; for it is time to be gracious to her, for the appointed time has come* (Psalm 102:1-2,13).

> *He looked upon their distress when He heard their cry; and He remembered His covenant for their sake, and relented according to the greatness of His lovingkindness. He also made them objects of compassion in the presence of all their captors. Save us, O Lord our God, and gather us from among the nations, to give thanks to Your holy name and glory in Your praise* (Psalm 106:44-47).

SCRIPTURES FOR PRAYER

- Genesis 12:1-3; 35:11-12
- Deuteronomy 30:1-4

- Psalms 102:1-2,13; 105; 106:44-47; 122:6; 137:4-6; 147:1-2

- Isaiah 11:10-12; 14:1-2; 27:12-13; 40:1-5; 41:8-11; 42:22; 43:1-13; 44:3-6; 45:2-6; 46:3-4; 49:8-10,22; 51:14; 57:18; 59:21; 60:4,8-9; 62:4-7;10-12

- Jeremiah 16:14-16; 23:3-8; 30:10,16-17; 31:7-11; 31-34,37

- Ezekiel 20:33-35; 34:11-16; 36:8,17–28;24-28; 37:12-14; 39:27-28

- Hosea 3–4; 11; 14

- Amos 9:11-14

- Micah 4:6-7

- Zephaniah 2:1-2,6-7

- Romans 11:11-12; 12:17-18; 15:27

- Ephesians 3:6

But you, Israel, My servant, Jacob whom I have chosen, descendant of Abraham My friend, you whom I have taken from the ends of the earth, and called from its remotest parts and said to you, "You are My servant, I have chosen you and not rejected you. Do not fear, for I am with you; do not anxiously look about you, for I am your God. I will strengthen you, surely I will help you, surely I will uphold you with My righteous right hand." Behold, all those who are angered at you will be shamed and dishonored; those who contend with you will be as nothing and will perish (Isaiah 41:8-11).

"As for Me, this is My covenant with them," says the Lord: "My Spirit which is upon you, and My words which I have put in your mouth shall not depart from your

mouth, nor from the mouth of your offspring, nor from the mouth of your offspring's offspring," says the Lord, "from now and forever" (Isaiah 59:21).

Join me and thousands of others around the globe as we enter into crisis intervention through the power of prayer and fasting. Yes, together we shall make history before the throne of the Almighty!

Appendix C

RESOURCES FOR INTERCESSORS

This is not an exhaustive list. On many of the recommended Websites, you will find links to other helpful organizations, as well as extensive lists of books about intercessory prayer and the Prayer Storm themes of prayer emphasis, revival, youth awakening, Israel, and crisis intercession.

24-7 PRAYER (WWW.24-7PRAYER.COM/ CM/RESOURCES/288)

Pete Greig, who formerly worked with Jackie Pullinger in Hong Kong, is now an author, a church-planter, and the international director of 24-7 Prayer, which has grown in eight years from a single 24-7 prayer room based on the Moravian model into an "international, interdenominational youth movement committed to prayer, mission and justice."

AGLOW INTERNATIONAL (WWW.AGLOW.ORG)

Since Aglow was formed in 1967, it has been known as a network of caring, praying women. Now 172 nations strong, Aglow can rapidly mobilize via e-mail more than one million intercessors worldwide who understand the power of strategic prayer.

BOUND4LIFE (HTTP://BOUND4LIFE.COM)

Along with others, pray a short prayer, frequently and effectively: "Jesus, I plead your blood over my sins and the sins of my nation; God, end abortion, and send revival to America." Participate in silent prayer "seiges." See Website for more information and for resources such as a prayer-reminder wristband.

THE CALL (WWW.THECALL.COM)

Spearheaded by Lou Engle, these are stadium events that are not merely concerts but are rather, in their words—"A fast, not a festival" and "a massive gathering of young and old who are desperate for a revival in our nation." On the Website, you will find a news feed, information about upcoming gatherings, resources, and more.

CAMPUS CHURCH NETWORKS (HTTP://CAMPUSCHURCH.NET)

CAMPUS TRANSFORMATION NETWORK (HTTP://CAMPUSTRANSFORMATION.COM)

Jaeson Ma (www.jaesonma.com) is a 20-something Chinese American with a passion for Jesus. He leads a growing campus ministry, and he is the author of *The Blueprint: A Revolutionary Plan to Plant Missional Communities on Campus.*

THE DAILY BRIEF (HTTP://CHPPONLINE.BLOGSPOT.COM/)

"The Daily Brief" is a daily news alert sent free by e-mail to subscribers. It is published by Capitol Hill Prayer Partners (CHPP), which is a ministry dedicated to praying for U.S. leaders and for issues involving national security. Their Website includes many links to other organizations and ministries.

DAILY TEXT (BIBLE VERSES AND PRAYERS FOR EACH DAY OF THE YEAR)

Bible texts are selected annually by the Moravian Church and shared world wide—since 1731! This rich source of personal renewal is produced fresh each year by praying and believing Moravian Christians. Order it in a book form or receive it free via e-mail.

> Mount Carmel Ministries
> 800 Mount Carmel Drive NE
> PO Box 579
> Alexandria, MN 56308
> Phone: 320-846-2744 or 1-800-793-4311
> Fax: 320-846-0067
> Website: www.dailytext.com

For an e-mail devotional version of Daily Text sent directly to you each day contact: ministries@dailytext.com

DAY TO PRAY FOR THE PEACE OF JERUSALEM (HTTP://EW.US.CHURCHINSIGHT.COM/GROUP/GROUP.ASPX?ID=1000001667)

The International Day of Prayer for the Peace of Jerusalem is held annually on the first Sunday of October, coinciding with the season of Yom Kippur. It is one of the initiatives of Eagles' Wings executive director Robert Stearns.

EVERY HOME FOR CHRIST (WWW.EHC.ORG)

Find books and other resources, such as a World Prayer Map, on their Website. Every Home for Christ and its Jericho Center of Prayer are chaired by national prayer leader Dick Eastman.

GLOBAL DAY OF PRAYER
(WWW.GLOBALDAYOFPRAYER.COM/)

From South Africa, Graham Powells coordinates a multi-nation day of prayer. The Website, which includes links to the GDoP sites of dozens of countries, gives details of past events and the current year's events. The key Scripture for the GDoP is Second Chronicles 7:14: "If my people, who are called by My name, will humble themselves and pray...."

HARVEST PRAYER MINISTRIES
(WWW.HARVESTPRAYER.COM)

Harvest Prayer Ministries was formed "to equip the local church to become a House of Prayer for all nations, releasing God's power for revival and finishing the task of world evangelization." Follow a link to an extensive online prayer-themed bookshop called PrayerShop.

INCREASE INTERNATIONAL
(WWW.INTERCESSORSINTERNATIONAL.ORG/)

Elizabeth (Beth) Alves assembles intercessors for teaching and united prayer. Her books include *Intercessors: Discovering Your Prayer Power and Becoming a Prayer Warrior.*

INTERCESSORS FOR AMERICA (WWW.IFAPRAY.ORG)

This site and free subscription-only e-mails contain a wealth of up-to-date information about national and international prayer needs, including those of Israel. IFA partners with many other organizations, and you can find links to their Web-sites on the IFA site, including the following sites which may be of particular interest to Prayer Storm intercessors: America's

National Prayer Committee, The U.S. Prayer Center, Mission America, Campus Renewal Ministries, See You at the Pole (youth), and more. Over 300 books about prayer and prayer-related issues are available through IFA.

INTERNATIONAL HOUSE OF PRAYER (IHOP)
(WWW.IHOP.ORG/GROUP/GROUP.ASPX?ID=14025)

From Kansas City, Missouri, Mike Bickle and his team coordinate 24/7 worship and intercession. The Web site is a rich source of prayer resources, including information about conferences, webcasts and podcasts, Nightwatch, the Israel Mandate, and the Global Bridegroom Fast.

ISRAEL PRAYER COALITION (WWW.ENCOUNTERSNETWORK.COM/
ISRAEL_PRAYER_COALITION)

James W. Goll networks with ministries of intercession, compassion, and humanitarian aid to Israel, coordinating and releasing strategic calls to prayer, including the The Cry (prayer and fasting during Purim each year). The Coalition also hosts prayer-focused tours to Israel.

JERUSALEM HOUSE OF PRAYER
FOR ALL NATIONS (WWW.JHOPFAN.ORG)

Tom Hess is the president of this organization, the motto of which is "Proclaim...Pray...Praise." He leads prayer tours of Israel, prayer convocations, the Watchman's School of Ministry, and the All Nations World Wide Watch Jerusalem, which proclaim, praise, and pray for the peace of Jerusalem through the twelve gates of the city.

LUKE 18 PROJECT (WWW.LUKE18PROJECT.COM)

Directed by Brian Kim and closely affiliated with TheCall (Lou Engle), the Luke 18 Project has a goal of planting 24/7 prayer rooms on every college campus—as many as 10,000 of them. It is based on Luke 18:6-7: "And the Lord said, ...'Will not God bring about justice for his chosen ones, who cry out to him day and night?'"

MOMS IN TOUCH (WWW.MOMSINTOUCH.ORG)

Founded and directed by Fern Nichols in 1984 and growing quickly because of exposure on Focus on the Family, today Moms In Touch has groups in all 50 states as well as representatives in over 120 foreign countries. They pray weekly for their children and their schools.

MORAVIAN HYMNS

Historic Moravian hymns have been translated into English. *The Moravian Book of Worship* is available from the Moravian Church (which celebrated its 550-year anniversary in 2007) at www.moravian.org/publications/catalog. *The Companion to the Moravian Book of Worship* is available from the Moravian Music Foundation at www.moravianmusic.org/books.html.

NATIONAL DAY OF PRAYER (WWW.NDPTF.ORG)

This national day of prayer for America's leaders and families exists because of a presidential decree, and it operates under the authority of the President of the United States. The National Day of Prayer itself is held annually on the first Thursday of May, and a year-round task force mobilizes participation and maintains communication.

NATIONAL GOVERNMENTAL PRAYER ALLIANCE (WWW.NATIONALGPA.ORG)

Established by Dutch Sheets, the NGPA networks with other Christian organizations and serves as a "clearinghouse for information on the activities of our three branches of government at the national and state levels, enabling the Body of Christ to pray more effectively and to act responsibly and proactively to see governmental change." They also teach about effective intercession, making "every attempt to be prophetic and proactive as opposed to responsive and defensive" in their prayer activities.

PRAYER CENTRAL (WWW.PRAYERCENTRAL.NET)

This is a Web-based source of inspiration and information about prayer for national and international concerns, Israel, and much more.

PRAYER MOUNTAIN (WWW.FGTV.ORG/N_ENGLISH/PRAYER/P_INDEX.ASP)

The Osanri Choi Ja-Shil Memorial Fasting Prayer Mountain, Osanri, Kyonggi Province, Korea was founded by David Yonggi Cho's Yoidi Full Gospel Church of Seoul, South Korea. The Prayer Mountain can accomodate up to 10,000 people at one time for private and corporate prayer. (See also www.davidcho.com/NewEng/PrayerMountain.asp.)

PRAYER STORM (WWW.PRAYERSTORM.COM)

Keep up with the latest postings from James W. Goll and the Prayer Storm team. Sign up for your hour of prayer. (After only the first two months, 1,400 intercessors from 40 nations have signed up, taking one hour of prayer per week. The goal is one million intercessors praying around the clock, around the world for specific crises, revival in the Church, a youth awakening, and Israel!)

REFORMATION PRAYER NETWORK (WWW.GENERALS.ORG)

Founded by Mike and Cindy Jacobs of Generals International (formerly Generals of Intercession), the Reformation Prayer Network pulls together the apostolic, prophetic, and intercessory movements to more effectively bring the transformational power of the Kingdom of God to earth today.

SUCCAT HALLEL (WWW.JERUSALEMPRAISE.COM)

Succat Hallel means "Tabernacle of Praise" in Hebrew, and since 1999, Rick and Patti Ridings have hosted 24/7 prayer and praise in the city of Jerusalem. The primary facility of Succat Hallel overlooks Mount Zion and the Old City of Jerusalem.

WATCH OF THE LORD (WWW.MAHESHCHAVDA.COM/WOTL.ASP)

This is a global prayer movement begun by Mahesh and Bonnie Chavda in 1995. Up to a thousand believers ("watchmen") gather at the Watch headquarters in Charlotte, North Carolina, every Friday night to spend the entire night in worship and prayer. Other locations host similar gatherings. Individuals can participate in the Watch of the Lord via webcast.

ENDNOTES

INTRODUCTION

1. Facts for this section have been gleaned from "Zinzendorf: the Count Without Borders," the official site of the Zinzendorf documentary series from the Comenius Foundation, at http://www.zinzendorf.com/countz.htm; and from Leslie K. Tarr, "The Prayer Meeting that Lasted 100 Years," *Christian History*, no. 1 (1997): http://www.ctlibrary.com/3263.

CHAPTER 1

1. William Walford, "Sweet Hour of Prayer" (1845).

2. *Merriam-Webster's Collegiate Dictionary*, 11th ed., s.v. "Prayer"; see also *Shorter Oxford English Dictionary, Sixth Edition*.

3. *Merriam-Webster's Collegiate Dictionary*, 11th ed., s.v. "Intercede."

4. "Entugchano"; see http://www.studylight.org/lex/grk/view.cgi?number=1793; this resource uses *Thayer's and Smith's Bible Dictionary* and the *Theological Dictionary of the New Testament*.

5. Ibid.

6. "Paga"; see http://www.studylight.org/lex/heb/view.cgi? number=06293; this resource uses the *Brown-Driver-Briggs-Gesenius Lexicon* and the *Theological Word Book of the Old Testament*.

CHAPTER 2

1. Ernest W. Blandy, "Where He Leads Me" (1890).

2. *Strong's Exhaustive Concordance of the Bible*, "embrimaomai," 1690.

3. Charles Haddon Spurgeon, *Twelve Sermons on Prayer* (London: Marshall, Morgan, & Scott, n.d.), 39.

4. "Nasa"; see http://www.studylight.org/lex/heb/view.cgi? number=05375.

5. *Strong's Exhaustive Concordance of the Bible*, "bastazo," 941.

6. "Anechomai"; see http://www.studylight.org/lex/grk/view.cgi?number=430.

7. Wesley Duewel, *Mighty Prevailing Prayer* (Grand Rapids, MI: Zondervan, 1990), 40-41.

CHAPTER 3

1. Edwin Hatch, "Breathe on Me, Breath of God" (1878).

2. *Merriam-Webster's Collegiate Dictionary*, 11th ed., s.v. "Conspire"; from Latin "conspirare." "Breathed" or "Naphach"; http://www.studylight.org/lex/heb/view.cgi?number=05301.

3. "Genos"; see http://www.studylight.org/lex/grk/view.cgi?number=1085.

3. Colin Dye, teaching notes, quoted in James W. Goll, *Revival Breakthrough Study Guide* (Franklin, TN: Encounters Network, 2000), 43.

4. Duncan Campbell, "Revival in the Hebrides (1949)" (1969), transcript available at *Shilohouse Ministries,* http://www.shilohouse.org/Hebrides_Revival.htm (accessed 19 April 2008).

5. The story of the Hebrides Revival has been published in many places. Many of these details came from the Campbell transcript.

6. J. Edwin Orr, "Prayer and Revival," at http://www.jedwinorr.com/prayer_revival.htm.

7. Charles Finney, for this description of revival, see "What a Revival of Religion Is," http://www.gospeltruth.net/1868Lect_on_Rev_of_Rel/68revlec01.htm.

8. From commentary on Isaiah 62:6-9; Matthew Henry, *Commentary on the Whole Bible, Vol. IV* (Isaiah to Malachi), 2nd ed., (Peabody, MA: Hendrickson Publishers, 1991).

9. Leonard Ravenhill, *Why Revival Tarries* (Bloomington, MN: Bethany House, 1979), 138.

10. E.M. Bounds, *The Necessity of Prayer* (Grand Rapids, MI: Baker Publishing Group, 1979), 63.

CHAPTER 9

1. John R. Colgan, "Mighty Army of the Young" (1891).

2. Jaeson Ma, *The Blueprint* (Ventura, CA: Regal, 2007), 35-36.

3. Stephen Ross, "Charles Thomas (C.T.) Studd," *Worldwide Missions: Mission Biographies* (2007), http://www.wholesomewords.org/missions/biostudd.html (accessed 21 April 2008).

4. "Campus Ministry Cambridge Style," *Christian History & Biography*, 88 (2005), 13. For more on this subject, consult these books: *Revival Fire,* by Wesley Duewel; *The Classics on Revival,* by Robert Backhouse; *Campus Aflame,* by J. Edwin Orr; and *Revival: Its Principles and Personalities,* by Winkie Pratney.

5. J. Edwin Orr, "Prayer and Revival," www.jedwinorr.com/prayer_revival.htm (accessed May 2007), quoted in Jaeson Ma, *The Blueprint.*

6. Steve Shadrach, "5 Students Who Changed the World," *Boundless Webzine* (2003), http://www.boundless.org/2002_2003/regulars/list_guy/a0000739.html (accessed 21 April 2008).

7. Paul Van Der Werf, "Haystack Reloaded: Could a Haystack Change the World Again?" *Student Volunteer Movement* 2, http://www.svm2.citymaker.com/haystackreloaded.html (accessed 21 April 2008).

8. Randy Matthews, "Didn't He," *Son of Dust* (Woodland Studios, Nashville, TN: Myrrh Records, 1973).

9. Adapted from Jaeson Ma, *The Blueprint,* 107-110.

CHAPTER 10

1. Samuel O. Cluff, "I Am Praying for You" (1860), music by Ira E. Sankey (1874).

2. David Wilkerson.

Chapter 11

1. Julia W. Howe, "Battle Hymn of the Republic" (1861).

2. Andrew Murray, *Helps to Intercession* (Fort Washington, PA: Christian Literature Crusade, 2007), Day 17.

3. Jack W. Hayford, *Prayer Is Invading the Impossible* (New York: Ballantine Books, 1983), 57.

4. Thomas Hooker, quoted in Bruce P. Stark, "Thomas Hooker," *Connecticut's Heritage Gateway*, www.ctheritage.org, quoted in Derek Prince, *Shaping History Through Prayer and Fasting* (New Kensington, PA: Whitaker House, 2002).

5. Thomas Hooker, quoted in Alden T. Vaughan, *The Puritan Tradition in America*, 1620-1730 (Lebanon, NH: University Press of New England, 1997), 84.

6. Daniel Webster, quoted in Prince, *Shaping History Through Prayer and Fasting*.

7. Charles Stanley, see http://www.eagleforum.org/court_watch/reports/2001/6-27-01/pray-for-govt-officials.shtml.

8. Dick Eastman.

Chapter 12

1. *The Antiphonary of Bangor*, an early Irish manuscript in the Ambrosian Library of Milan (London: Harrison and Sons, 1893), 24.

2. "Energeo"; http://www.studylight.org/lex/grk/view.cgi?number=1754.

3. Joel Brinkley, "Ethiopian Jews and Israelis Exult as Airlift Is Completed," *The New York Times*, May 26, 1991,

http://query.nytimes.com/gst/fullpage.html?res=
9D0CE2DD1E3CF935A15756C0A967958260&sec=&spon=
&pagewanted=all (accessed 22 March 2008).

CONCLUSION

1. Julie Meyer, *Invitation to Encounter: A Journey in Dreams* (Kansas City, MO: Forerunner, 2008).

2. Eleanor A. Schroll, "The Beautiful Garden of Prayer" (1920).

ABOUT THE AUTHOR

James (Jim) W. Goll is the cofounder of Encounters Network (formerly Ministry to the Nations) with his wife, Michal Ann. James also acts as the director of Prayer Storm, an internet-based virtual house of prayer. They are members of the Harvest International Ministries Apostolic Team and contributing writers for *Kairos* magazine and other periodicals. James and Michal Ann have four wonderful children and live in the beautiful, rolling hills of Franklin, Tennessee.

James has produced several study guides on subjects such as Equipping in the Prophetic, Blueprints for Prayer, and Empowered for Ministry, which are all available through the Encounters Resource Center.

Other books by James and Michal Ann Goll include:

A Call to Courage
Angelic Encounters
Call to the Secret Place
Compassion
The Beginner's Guide to Hearing God
The Coming Israel Awakening
The Coming Prophetic Revolution
The Prophetic Intercessor
Praying for Israel's Destiny

For more information, contact:

Encounters Network
PO Box 1653
Franklin, TN 37057
Office Phone: 615-599-5552
Office Fax: 615-599-5554
For orders call: 1-877-200-1604

For more information or to sign up for monthly e-mail communiqués, please visit www.encountersnetwork.com or send an e-mail to: info@encountersnetwork.com.

For more information on Prayer Storm, visit www. prayerstorm.com. You may sign up for an hour of prayer or view the weekly Webcast by visiting this Website.

Additional copies of this book and other
book titles from DESTINY IMAGE are
available at your local bookstore.

Call toll-free: 1-800-722-6774.

Send a request for a catalog to:

Destiny Image® Publishers, Inc.
P.O. Box 310
Shippensburg, PA 17257-0310

*"Speaking to the Purposes of God for This
Generation and for the Generations to Come."*

For a complete list of our titles,
visit us at www.destinyimage.com.